"PLEASE, HONEY, DON'T KILL ME. I'M YOUR MOTHER!"

A terrified Mary Anne Woodham ran into her bedroom and tried to lock the door, but she wasn't strong enough to hold it closed.

Her sixteen-year-old son, Luke, forced his way in. He smashed his aluminum baseball bat down on a chest of drawers and then swung at a dresser as Mary Anne cowered on the double bed. She had no place to hide.

Woodham looked at his mother crying and pleading, crunched up in her pink jogging pants and sweatshirt. Closing his eyes, he lifted the bat up above his head and crashed it across his mother's face with the force of a runaway train. It fractured her jaw. Dropping the bat, he forced a pillow over her face and plunged the long blade of a hickory knife into her body, wildly stabbing and slashing at her over and over again until she died.

Finished with his work at home, Woodham grabbed his father's favorite hunting rifle. It was time to go to school.

BOOK YOUR PLACE ON OUR WEBSITE AND MAKE THE READING CONNECTION!

We've created a customized website just for our very special readers, where you can get the inside scoop on everything that's going on with Zebra, Pinnacle and Kensington books.

When you come online, you'll have the exciting opportunity to:

- View covers of upcoming books
- Read sample chapters
- Learn about our future publishing schedule (listed by publication month *and author*)
- Find out when your favorite authors will be visiting a city near you
- Search for and order backlist books from our online catalog
- Check out author bios and background information
- Send e-mail to your favorite authors
- Meet the Kensington staff online
- Join us in weekly chats with authors, readers and other guests
- Get writing guidelines
- AND MUCH MORE!

**Visit our website at
http://www.pinnaclebooks.com**

CHILD'S PREY

Jon Bellini

PINNACLE BOOKS
Kensington Publishing Corp.

http://www.pinnaclebooks.com

PINNACLE BOOKS are published by

Kensington Publishing Corp.
850 Third Avenue
New York, NY 10022

All Kensington Titles, Imprints, and Distributed Lines are available at special quantity discounts for bulk purchases for sales promotions, premiums, fund-raising, and educational or institutional use. Special book excerpts or customized printings can also be created to fit specific needs. For details, write or phone the office of the Kensington special sales manager: Kensington Publishing Corp., 850 Third Avenue, New York, NY 10022, attn: Special Sales Department, Phone: 1-800-221-2647.

Pinnacle and the P logo Reg. U.S. Pat. & TM Off.

First Printing: July 2001
10 9 8 7 6 5 4 3 2 1

Printed in the United States of America

*Dedicated to parents everywhere
who've given their children
all the love and attention they deserve*

"He who smites his father or mother shall surely be put to death."

—Exodus 21:15

Prologue

Pearl, Mississippi, 7:45 A.M., October 1, 1997

The sun peeped through a thin haze of cloud, casting a warm orange glow across the sprinklers watering the grass verges that bordered the Pearl High School parking lot. Dozens of students strolled across the blacktop toward the tall double doors that led to the school commons area. Many of the teenagers had Bibles in their arms because they'd just been to early morning prayer.

No one noticed the pale-faced, overweight teen driving the white Corsica to the far corner of the parking lot. He pulled up, sat alone and unsmiling. He glanced across at the students and teachers entering the high school.

The sixteen-year-old youth's gaze fixed on a student in her mid-teens. She was tall and shapely, her hair long and dark. She walked with a confident swagger. She was smiling.

As she went through the double doors into the Commons, the teen in the Corsica opened his door and headed across the parking lot.

At that moment another sixteen-year-old walked into the Commons with his buddy, a seventeen-year-old senior. The two boys settled at the spot where they sat every morning before classes began.

The overweight sixteen-year-old shuffled into the Commons area long enough to hand some notebooks to another boy, telling him to make sure he gave the notebooks to another older ex-student they both knew, then headed back out toward the parking lot.

The boy who'd just been handed the notebooks told a friend standing next to him that something very bad was about to happen. They moved down the corridor toward the library away from the Commons. The tubby teen walked back through the swinging doors like a cowboy about to challenge all comers to a saloon bar duel, a .30–.30 Marlin hunting rifle rested casually on his hip.

He approached two girls. The bubbly brunette he'd watched earlier looked up. The lone gunman was aiming his weapon straight at her, tears welling up in his eyes.

She instantly recognized the look of despair in his face and turned to run.

He squeezed the trigger and caught her in the back with two blasts before she'd gotten two steps away. The sound of the shots echoed around the large hallway. Students began screaming. One fourteen-year-old ninth grader and a friend began running. The lone gunman aimed and fired at them. The bullet ricocheted off a brick post as they scrambled for cover.

The shooter aimed again at the fourteen-year-old ninth grader. A beat later the teen heard the bullet hit his book bag with a thud before it dropped to the floor and literally exploded.

The gunman swung his weapon toward another girl student who'd been standing near his first victim. As she scrambled away, he shot her in the head. After the bullet struck, her eyes rolled back in her head and she fell to the floor.

A seventeen-year-old junior turned and ran for her life, but in the confusion ran straight into a wall. That was when she felt the severe pain in her left shoulder where a bullet had hit her. She scrambled back to her feet and made it to the bathroom across the hall, where she huddled and cried, too afraid to open the door.

Students and school staff continued running for cover behind pillars, tables, chairs—anything that might protect them from the onslaught.

By now the lone gunman was firing randomly in all directions, his weapon still resting on his hip.

When the young shooter stopped to reload his rifle, one brave student tried to tackle him. He ran after the teen, grabbed him, and they grappled for a few seconds until the gunman shoved him to the ground and headed across the hall, his rifle resting on his hip again.

On the other side of the hall, a sports coach directed students out of the building. One seventeen-year-old senior helped another injured classmate to safety, taking off his own shirt to try and stop the wounded student's bleeding.

The gunman shouted wildly in the direction of one male senior, "You turned your back on us." Then he shot straight at the student's hip. He instantly fell to the ground.

Out in the parking lot, other students heard the blasts and thought it was the cannon used at school football games.

One junior was struck by a bullet in the left side of

her stomach. She fell to the ground screaming for her friend. As two other girls ran for their lives, they dropped school bags and one of them even lost one of her sneakers in the panic. Filled with an impending sense of doom, the two teens headed for a small wood beyond the parking lot and kept running.

Back in the commons area, bullets were striking the black-and-white floor and fragmenting before grazing students in the legs as they ran for cover.

One seventeen-year-old sophomore leaped in front of his girlfriend to try and shield her. He took gunshot wounds to both legs and crashed to the floor.

The gunman walked over to the sophomore to say he was sorry. He'd thought the student was someone else.

The lone gunman began firing again.

A fourteen-year-old freshman stumbled toward the school's band hall. It was only when a friend took a look at his leg that he realized he'd been hit in the left calf.

Bullets ripped through lockers and chipped powder kegs of plaster off the walls as they ricocheted in all directions.

The lone gunman stopped almost as suddenly as he had begun. A cloud of dust and cordite wafted through the wall of silence that descended on the scene of carnage.

Gazing through the mist at the bloodshed he had just created, the shooter pointed the barrel down, turned around and shuffled back out of the school.

The community of Pearl, in Rankin County, Mississippi, would never be the same again.

PART I

LIFE

"No one else took care of him.
When he cried, I held him.
When he was in trouble,
I helped him when no one else did."

—Grant Boyette

One

Rankin County, Mississippi, was formed in 1828 and named after onetime Congressional representative Christopher Rankin. The county was the twenty-fifth of Mississippi's eighty-two counties to be created.

In the 1860s, a small number of people migrated to an area of Rankin County, adjacent to the Pearl River. It was good farming land in those days and homesteaders would catch fish for their dinner and grow their corn in the fields. The area became known as Pearl. It didn't develop much in those days because the river wasn't suitable for boats.

In the mid-1950s, Pearl changed from rural to suburban—thanks to a huge influx of postwar industry in the area, and residents from the nearby state capital of Jackson who bought land and built houses so they could live outside the busy metropolis. Between 1960 and 1970, the population of Pearl shot up by a vast 89.4 percent, making it one of the top-ten, fastest-growing cities in the Magnolia State. So many people were flooding into the area that the local newspaper issued a special issue called *The Pearl Press Newcomer's Edition*.

Pearl had become a magnet for people from all over the state because of its reputation as a safe environment, and it was in the middle of all this rapid growth that a young trainee accountant named John P. Woodham II first spotted Pearl's potential. Woodham, from the Mississippi community of Newton, forty miles to the east of Pearl, was a Mississippi boy through and through. His family had lived in Newton for three generations since arriving from England in the late 1800s. He wanted to escape them and start a new, independent adult life of his own in a safe and secure environment because he intended to one day marry and have a family.

When Woodham arrived in Pearl in 1965, he was mightily impressed by its sporting grounds, brand-new stores, and the auto parks that lined the newly developing main strip on the old 20 Highway. Pearl was proud of being one of the few places where trailers had their own landscaped gardens and were set in picturesque parks in the middle of the community. In Newton, trailer parks meant trashy folk in trashy locations, and not a lot else.

Woodham liked Pearl's proud conceit that it had no social or class boundaries because it had pretty much been developed simultaneously. Pearl was a model community for the entire state. It had little crime—a safe place to live and raise your kids. And Woodham's qualifications as a fully trained accountant made him just the type of professional Pearl wanted as part of its drive to become a fully incorporated city.

John Woodham met and started dating a pretty girl of twenty, eight years his junior. The wonders of Pearl were one of their most popular topics of conversation.

Woodham soon fell head over heels in love with Mary Anne, a bubbly blonde with a good figure and an infectious laugh.

"John and Mary Anne were so happy with each

other. They seemed like the perfect couple," recalled one old family friend Margaret Fuller.

In 1967, John and Mary Anne got married and it looked as if their American dream was just beginning.

The Woodhams chose a brand-new, spacious, three-bedroom house in a quiet street just a quarter of a mile from the Pearl Police Station. It seemed an ideal, safe environment.

The Woodhams appeared to friends and relatives as the ideal couple, even if their characters were somewhat different. He was quiet and reserved, and she was louder, more positive.

"They say opposites attract and that's what we all felt about John and Mary Anne. They seemed so at ease with each other," recalled Margaret Fuller.

But settling into Pearl in those heady early days when its growth rate was higher than any other community in the state was not quite as easy as the Woodhams had thought.

John would go off to his accountant's job back on I-20 in Newton while Mary Anne was left at home to amuse herself. The idea had been to start a family as soon as possible, but as is sometimes the case, it was easier said than done.

After less than a year of living in Pearl, Mary Anne found that without a family it got pretty boring. She couldn't even pop out and buy herself a beer or a bottle of wine because Pearl was a dry town in those days. It would be another ten years before beer and wine were even allowed to be sold in selected stores and restaurants. The ban on hard liquor has never been lifted.

"Back in those early days, you had to drive fifty miles out into the country to even get yourself a beer," explained long-time Pearl Police Department Officer George Burgess.

There wasn't any place full of friendly people where Mary Anne could go shopping, either. Pearl had deliberately not built itself a downtown area like the older communities because it wanted to discourage people—especially teenagers—from loitering on streets. It preferred that churches and malls be built on the edge of the city.

In those early days the most common crime was speeding. Even burglaries were a rarity and street crime was nonexistent. Back then the Pearl Police Department experienced its only face-off in living memory when a bunch of bank robbers had a shootout. But it ended peacefully and no one was hurt.

Mary Anne had a big problem with the way Pearl was promoted as a young person's paradise, because there wasn't anything for a young person to do.

Mary Anne Woodham ended her boredom by enrolling in a local teacher-training college. Two years later, she qualified as a substitute teacher to kindergarten kids. The job was only part-time, which pleased John Woodham because he was convinced his young wife would get pregnant eventually.

It took a long time for their patience to be rewarded. As the Mississippi Supreme Court was finally granting Pearl its city status in 1973, Mary Anne got pregnant. It had been six years since their wedding. Later in 1973, Mary Anne gave birth to a boy they named John P. Woodham III.

* * *

It was only natural that after such a long wait, the Woodhams would both heap loving care and attention on their firstborn child.

John Woodham was earning a decent wage as an accountant, so Mary Anne Woodham even gave up her part-time job for a while to make sure that the baby got her full-time attention. Naturally, she spoiled him.

Those who encountered the proud parents back in those days recall them as being a striking couple. Mary Anne, with her sometimes blond, sometimes brunette well-styled hair, and the more reserved, tall, upstanding, bespectacled John seemed well matched. They and their baby were just the sort of folk Pearl was proud to have in the community. A responsible, caring family was how many described the Woodhams in those days.

At home, Mary Anne waited until little John was in kindergarten before going back to her part-time job as a teacher. But she always made sure she dropped off and picked up her child from school every day.

Friends at the time recall Mary Anne as being over-protective toward her son.

"She sorta smothered that kid. She adored him like most parents, but she acted like she owned him at times," said one old friend, Geena Cox.

Mary Anne was also obsessed with other aspects of her parental responsibilities, like bathing and eating.

"She wouldn't let anyone come 'round the house at a certain time each day because she had to give John a bath at a very precise time," added Cox.

Mary Anne Woodham told one friend at the time that she'd seen so many neglected kids, even in the kindergartens of Pearl, that she was determined to protect her own child, no matter what.

She took little John to the local Baptist church every Sunday, but her husband rarely made an appearance. He was not particularly religious, but was happy to let his wife get involved with the church. Mary Anne wanted her son to grow up as a caring, loving Christian, and made sure he said his prayers before every meal and just before he went to bed each night.

John and Mary Anne Woodham soon became keen to add another child to their family. They didn't want little John growing up without a brother or sister.

"Mary Anne was determined to have another child. She used to say that single kids had the worst of both worlds. She really did care," explained Geena Cox.

But Mary Anne was to go through the same heartbreaking gap she had experienced trying to get pregnant the first time.

"It was almost as if God was telling her that really she wasn't cut out to have kids," said Cox.

But Mary Anne was nothing if not determined. She'd gotten pregnant before and she'd manage it again, however long it took.

Inevitably, the strain of trying to have another child caused a few cracks to appear in the Woodhams' marriage. John was trying to hold down a job, and Mary Anne was expecting him to whisk her off to bed virtually from the moment he walked through the door each evening.

It took almost seven years from the day of her first child's birth in 1973 for Mary Anne to get pregnant.

On February 5, 1981, Mary Anne produced another bouncing baby boy, christened Luke Timms.

The Woodhams' American dream was still on course—even if the age gap between the boys was a little wide.

Two

A sign in front of Mary Anne Woodham's favorite church, the First Baptist in Pearl, read OPEN WIDE YOUR HEARTS. It symbolized everything about the close-knit Mississippi community and her attitude toward it.

By the time little Luke came on the scene, Pearl had an enviable reputation as the thirteenth largest city in the state (population almost 20,000), was renowned for its churches, secure family environment, recreation, award-winning schools, the annual Pearl Day festival, and rapid business and industrial growth.

Even Pearl's climate seemed tailor-made for the Woodhams, with an overall average temperature of a comfortable 65 degrees, with an average winter temperature of 46.5 degrees and an average summer of 79.1 degrees.

"And you could count the number of violent crimes in those days on one hand," said local cop George Burgess. "I guess it was the nearest to perfection you can find in a community."

By the mid-1980s Pearl was home to three elementary schools, a junior high and high school, plus the Rankin branch of Hinds Junior College. There was also an award-winning library and a central city-park softball complex.

John Woodham got himself a more high-powered job at the City of Pearl audit offices.

Pearl—now with 800 businesses, 6,000 houses, and 1,300 apartment buildings—was a busy metropolis and John Woodham found himself working harder than ever before. By that time, the city boasted municipal services including police, fire, street lighting, water and waste systems, four city parks, small animal control, and emergency medical response. It all meant nonstop juggling of facts and figures for John Woodham in his new job.

The city had generous facilities and youth-oriented programs. It encouraged parents to do the work, but unfortunately John Woodham was so busy running things he didn't have much time to help. Mary Anne Woodham, thirty-four by the time little Luke was born, couldn't have been happier. She continued to hold down her part-time job as a substitute teacher in the Pearl school district. It was a perfect career, because it meant that she very rarely had to leave Luke or his brother, John, with baby-sitters.

Mary Anne was renowned at Pearl kindergartens for being extremely protective of all children. She was always asking them awkward questions to try to get a handle on whether they had any problems at home.

Other teachers felt at the time that Mary Anne sometimes went too far in her interrogation of the pupils. "It was as if she was looking for problems that didn't really exist—but we all reckoned she had her heart in the right place," explained a former teaching colleague, Jayme Driver.

Back at home, baby Luke had become the apple of his mom's eye, while little John faced the "older child" syndrome of being expected to fend for himself. What Mary Anne did not seem to realize was that the age gap between her sons meant that John had suddenly found himself relegated to the subs' bench.

"You can't just switch affection to another child after seven years—and expect the older one not to get upset," explained child-care specialist Peter Lugg. "It's not surprising that he grew to resent his baby brother. And sometimes that resentment can grow into real hatred."

While Mary Anne Woodham didn't seem to notice the problems between her son John and his younger brother, others did.

"They just weren't close. I guess the age gap didn't help, but you never felt they were truly brothers in the real sense of the word. They never laughed together," remembered Geena Cox.

Luke claimed many years later that John got his revenge by secretly punching him as he lay in his cot, or tripping him up in the backyard when no one was looking.

When Luke went running to his mom for protection from his older brother, Mary Anne saw it as being nothing more serious than a bit of sibling rivalry.

However, the problem soon escalated. By the time Luke was three, his ten-year-old brother had gotten into the habit of holding his hand out against Luke's head and encouraging him to try to punch him. Luke did not have the reach and it was a taunting, highly frustrating scenario for the little boy.

It was an image that would haunt Luke Woodham in later years.

* * *

Gradually, Luke Woodham grew into an active child, but he had the irritating habit of being very clumsy and was often shouted at by Mary Anne for knocking over things.

But there were far more worrying elements appearing on the surface of the Woodhams' "perfect" life in that "perfect" community of Pearl. Mary Anne's husband, John, was starting to feel he'd been left out of the proceedings. The birth of Luke had been a truly wonderful event for the family, but the child seemed to be taking up so much of his mother's time and attention that it wasn't just brother John who was feeling left out of the loop.

Unfortunately, John Woodham did not find it easy to put his feelings into words and for at least a year he did nothing to confront the issue with his wife. Instead, he went into long, silent sulks for days on end, which enormously frustrated the gregarious, outgoing Mary Anne because she didn't know what the problem was.

Running the household and working meant she didn't really have time to pander to her husband's moods. She always had other things to do—shopping, washing, gardening, cleaning the house. The result was that John and Mary Anne started arguing with alarming regularity. Not only to the detriment of their own relationship, but their two sons were exposed to a lot of screaming matches.

The atmosphere in the house rapidly deteriorated. John Woodham started working later and later at night to avoid all the issues. He was under intense pressure at work, which meant he was far from relaxed when he did finally get home each evening.

Often he'd walk in through the front door to be

greeted by chaos because Mary Anne hadn't had time to clean the house between feeding the children, washing all their clothes, and holding down her job. None of it was conducive to a relaxed home environment. John Woodham found life at the office much easier.

As gossip about the Woodhams' stormy relationship began circulating through the neighborhood, fewer and fewer parents were prepared to allow their children to visit the family home. On the few occasions when the younger John and Luke went around to other children's houses, the two boys would often get very aggressive if they didn't get their own way.

"It was obvious these two kids were not happy. They were plain destructive with other children's toys. It didn't make them real popular round here," said Geena Cox.

Very rapidly, the Woodhams were starting to isolate themselves from the rest of the community. But that was only the beginning.

There is no doubt John Woodham was a good, loving father to little Luke and his big brother, John, but the rows and arguments were driving him away. Mary Anne, trying to hold down her teaching job and look after two small, demanding children, began dreading spending any time alone with her husband. Eventually, she began going out at night with friends, and leaving little John to baby-sit his kid brother. That simply gave the older boy a chance to exact even more physical revenge on his "spoiled" brother.

The once mellow, reserved John P. Woodham II began harboring a lot of resentments about his life—and took them out on his wife. He accused Mary Anne of

showing favoritism toward Luke, which caused even
more problems in the home because Mary Anne insisted on dragging both boys into the room to listen
to their father's tirade of verbal abuse. John also objected to the way his wife was often out partying when
he got home late. After all, she was supposed to be
the mother of his children.

As the truth of the situation began to dawn on Mary
Anne, she started blaming her kids—especially Luke—
for the problems in her marriage. Then in a pang of
guilt she'd overcompensate by smothering him in
kisses and cuddles. Being an emotional punching bag,
torn between his mother and father, was an extremely
confusing and distressing experience for Luke Woodham.

By the time the big day came for Luke's arrival at
kindergarten, he was terrified of meeting his classmates because he'd encountered so few children of his
own age.

Not only had some of his parents' harsh words made
him feel their marriage problems were his fault, but
he'd already convinced himself that no other children
would want to play with him or even know him. After
all, his most impressionable experience of other kids
had been his big brother's punching him in the stomach or tripping him in the backyard.

Within days of starting kindergarten, Luke was being
bullied and terrorized by a section of his class. They
teased him about his goofy haircut and how his mom
made him wear shorts, even in the winter.

Trey Bynum went through the entire Pearl school
system with Luke. They weren't proper friends—Wood-

ham didn't have one—but Trey played with Luke on a regular basis.

"He was always picked on by the other boys. They called him every name under the sun," Bynum later recalled. "It was tough for Luke."

As all the screaming continued inside the Woodham home, little Luke found solace and comfort with numerous pets, including two cats, a dog called Sparkle, and a snake. His parents had recognized the need to provide the shy, awkward little boy with something to love and cherish.

The youngster spent hours every day in the backyard nurturing and talking to his animals. They all seemed far more agreeable than human beings. And they didn't say hurtful things to him.

Three

In the mid-1980s, all John Woodham's hard work at the office and long hours paid off when he landed a plum accounting job as assistant comptroller in a neighboring county. It was a more high-pressure position, but the improved salary, he hoped, might help ease tensions at home.

Nothing could have been further from the truth. Family friend Geena Cox explained, "Mary Anne ran a chaotic household. She was always screaming and shouting at the boys and John was such a quiet kinda guy he seemed to find it difficult to cope."

John Woodham's problems at home were distracting him from his job, and within a short period of time Woodham was fired for poor performance. It was a terrible blow to the shy, quiet-spoken Woodham. His self-confidence crumbled virtually overnight.

Although he had quite substantial savings, Woodham was loathe to dip into what he considered an insurance policy for their old age.

To make matters worse, Mary Anne had to put up with him sitting around the house all day, sulking and refusing to do any household chores, and constantly criticizing her.

Woodham often spent days at home shut away in his

tiny study, talking to no one. Even his beloved son Luke found it virtually impossible to raise a smile from his troubled dad.

The rows inside the house grew steadily worse because of John Woodham's refusal to try to find another job. The only light relief came when John Woodham took Luke to the ballpark or even more occasionally, chucked a few balls through the hoop in the backyard.

But Mary Anne feared it was only a matter of time before it all completely fell apart.

"Mary Anne knew there were big problems between them," said Geena Cox. "She told me she was miserable with him."

In 1987—when Luke Woodham was just seven years old—his father walked out on the family. It wasn't a surprise, but it deepened the feeling of isolation felt by the young boy.

Luke later claimed his life had been easygoing until the moment his dad left the family home. Even the way his brother beat him didn't ruin it. But his parents' big, final split was catastrophic.

Luke was in second grade when his dad, as he put it years later, "left the rest of the family to fend for themselves."

His mother, Mary Anne, remained behind running the family home single-handedly. She ruled the house with a practical hand, but it was difficult.

Mary Anne had little time to give her children individual attention. She'd get up in the morning, cook the breakfast, throw the dirty clothes in the washing machine, make sure her boys were dressed properly for school, and check their book bags for homework.

Then she'd bundle them into her car, drive them each to their schools—and then get to work for an eight A.M. start. Work seemed like a vacation to Mary Anne compared with what she had to do at home.

It was hardly surprising she frequently sought solace with a glass of wine or beer in the company of a few friends. Older son, John, was already staying out late at night, escaping the chaos of the Woodham house. But Luke remained alone at home for hours on end, or trapped in the living room watching TV with his increasingly overbearing mom.

Mary Anne started to get very frustrated with Luke because he was so unresponsive to her. She wanted a son she could talk to about things, but Luke answered all her questions with a simple yes or no—and he never elaborated about his feelings.

With his severe crew cut, thick brown glasses, and awkward demeanor, Luke stood out in a crowd for all the wrong reasons. On the mantelpiece of the Woodhams' living room was a family photo of Luke, his mom, and brother, John. Luke's chubby face smiled unsurely at the camera. Luke hated that photo from the moment he saw it and would try to remove it from the living room at every opportunity. To him, it was a false representation of an apparently happy family. As he later insisted, he never recovered his happiness after his dad walked out.

In the school yard, most kids found Luke's shy, almost manic habit of always staring very irritating. When he did find a playmate, it didn't last long because Luke refused to share things with other children.

Already his self-esteem was disturbingly low. He was

afraid of people. Afraid of the outside world. Luke had always been close to both his parents. But it was his mother who'd protected him and showered him with the most love and affection. And the moment his dad left it all seemed to disappear.

Luke Woodham suffered frequent pangs of guilt as do many children after their parents separate or divorce. Subconsciously, he was blaming himself for the fact that his mom was now bringing the family up alone.

Mary Anne Woodham, with her hair always neatly styled, sparkly brown eyes, and penchant for natty, pink jogging pants and sweatshirts, tried to put a brave face on things. But she was fighting an uphill struggle trying to cope with the relentless juggling of being a single parent.

Mary Anne continued to wear her wedding band in the hope that she might one day get back with John. But he did little to encourage that notion and very quickly became a rare visitor to the family home in Pearl.

Luke was distraught about not seeing his beloved dad. It seemed that John Woodham couldn't face up to the very people he'd once adored so much.

Luke's older brother was just as upset about the split. He was in many ways more immediately affected by the breakup because he was older and more worldly. He also felt a lot of bitterness toward his mother for the way she had spoiled his kid brother.

But as Luke grew older, he felt his mom slipping away from him as a person. She was so preoccupied with running the family, working and unwinding with her friends at night that she just didn't seem to have time for a proper relationship with her youngest son anymore.

"I guess I really didn't have much of one [a relationship] with her," he later recalled. " And, you know, I mean, we never really got along. And she always deserted me and left me out. And, and she just, I guess it just wasn't really good."

While Luke Woodham would later insist his mother had neglected to carry out many of her parental duties, others had a completely different impression of Mary Anne.

Sherrilyn Friend became closely acquainted with Mary Anne Woodham when they met at the Park Place Baptist Church in Pearl. The two women were in the same Sunday school class. Friend never forgot how Mary Anne and her older son, John, helped her and her pregnant daughter move into the Eastville apartment block just next to the Woodham house on Barrow Street. Soon they were regularly visiting each other's homes.

To Friend, Mary Anne Woodham was a decent, hardworking single mom who was trying desperately to keep her family intact.

"It was tough for her but she always managed to keep things together," Friend later explained. "She always had a smile on her face and a good word to say about everyone."

Inside the Woodham home, Mary Anne introduced "food rules" that were a recipe for disaster for a child like Luke. They went far beyond what most parents would consider strict, much less practical or effective.

Mary Anne Woodham hated any food being wasted.

One time, just after his father had left home, Luke poured some remainders in the garbage and his mom went berserk.

"She picked them all out again and made him eat them because she couldn't stand the waste," confided a family friend.

Mary Anne did the same sort of thing a few years later when she caught Luke smoking one of her cigarettes. She made him smoke two packs all in succession until he was literally sick on the floor.

Even before he'd reached his teens, Mary Anne tried to maintain a strict control over her son's bedroom. She'd hold regular room inspections and fine him part of his allowance if it wasn't spotlessly clean.

One day Luke failed to clean his room and his mom collected all his toys and clothes and dumped them in the trash. Luke tried to retrieve the items, but she made him put them back in the trash a second time.

Luke later claimed that his mother yelled at him about something virtually every night of the week. No wonder, even at that young age, he preferred the solitude of his bedroom to watching TV or sitting anywhere near his mom—if she happened to be in for the evening.

In 1992, John and Mary Anne Woodham's marriage came to a legal end after twenty-five years. Luke hadn't even reached his teens. Divorce papers filed at the local Rankin County Chancery Court at the time show that Mary Anne had been a single mother for years before the final divorce settlement. She'd retained custody of Luke and her firstborn son, John P. Woodham III, throughout.

* * *

One of Luke's early classmates, Kacy Strauss, lived across the street from the Woodham family. On the few occasions she spoke to Luke, he made it clear he was mightily frustrated by his parents' divorce.

"Luke didn't really do anything after that," Strauss later recalled. "Luke was quiet. If he applied himself he could have been valedictorian. But he kept himself to himself and let the whole divorce thing get to him."

Many of the Woodhams' neighbors felt genuinely sorry for Mary Anne, who was holding down a full-time job and raising her two sons alone.

Neighbor Medgie Swann could see the Woodhams' backyard from her house in the next street. She frequently watched Mary Anne escape to her beloved rose bed after a furious argument with Luke about mowing the lawn.

"He would just do one or two strips," recalled Swann. "Or cut a square section in the middle of the yard. I got the impression he was a little rebellious toward his mother."

Mary Anne Woodham also had serious money problems. Her part-time job as a substitute teacher in the Pearl school district didn't earn her enough to single-handedly support her children and she received only a small amount from her husband. She needed something more lucrative following the divorce so she took a full-time job as a receptionist for Cal-Maine Foods in Pearl. Mary Anne settled in well at Cal-Maine Foods. She rapidly gained a reputation as a solid, reliable employee who hardly ever missed a day's work.

One staff member recalled: "Mary Anne had a smile for everyone. She seemed a really decent person."

Luke soon grew resentful of his mother's job because he had to go to school early as she had to be at work by seven A.M. It also meant that a lot of the domestic chores, like cleaning the house and doing the wash, were neglected simply because Mary Anne didn't have enough time in the day to get everything done.

Mary Anne was often out nights partying, leaving him alone, which further compounded his feelings of loneliness. Sometimes she didn't get back until dawn the following morning having left Luke home alone in a dingy, increasingly messy household with nothing but jumbo packs of chips and cookies to eat.

Luke—not yet in his teens—was very confused by his mom's behavior. On the one hand, she and her two children were still regulars at the local Baptist church. On the other, at night she was behaving strangely, coming home at all hours.

Although she sometimes persuaded Luke's bigger brother, now in his teens, to baby-sit, John was still partial to using his kid brother as a punching bag whenever it took his fancy. Luke encouraged his mother to leave him alone at night rather than face up to his big brother.

By the time Luke got to junior high, he was at least twenty pounds overweight and faced a barrage of nicknames from "fat" to "chunky" to "chubby."

"And those were the better ones," recalled Trey Bynum, one of the few children to witness Luke's progress right through the Pearl school system.

Explained Bynum, "The stronger kids used to jump him [start fights] all the time. Everybody picked on him. I felt real sorry for him."

Luke Woodham's beloved pets in the backyard of

the family home had become the only living things he truly loved. For hours he would throw sticks to the end of the yard and encourage his dog, Sparkle, to catch them and bring them back to him.

It was his only escape. . . .

Four

Pearl High School was considered the jewel of the community. Locals believed educational standards in Pearl were higher than anywhere else in the country because they had the best teachers. In turn, the parents of Pearl students were renowned for lending their support to every single aspect of high school life.

"The first PTA meeting I went to had one thousand people," said parent Jim Lott, who was minister of music and activities at the First Baptist Church. "You don't get that kinda support elsewhere."

Unfortunately Luke Woodham's life couldn't have been further removed from that dreamscape scenario. He already hated school because he was picked on and the nearest his mom got to a PTA meeting was dropping Luke off at school every morning.

On Luke's first day at Pearl High School, he faced up to all the traditional freshman's traps with a mixture of fear and trepidation. Most new students didn't take more than a few days at Pearl High School to work out ways to avoid the ridicule of the notorious Freshman Loop, or to find the politically correct place to stand in the Commons. But the whole process was a nightmare come true for shy, geeky Luke Woodham.

The Freshman Loop was the circular drive in front of the school entrance where parents dropped off their nondriving teens. It was a prime location for chiding rookie students. Enterprising kids soon learned how to avoid that "stigma" by getting dropped off at the end of the sidewalk and then hitching a ride to the front door with the "cool dudes"—the students with cars.

But fat, bespectacled Luke Woodham didn't even have that choice because his mother, Mary Anne, insisted on taking her son right up to the doors of the entrance. That meant all his classmates could see him dutifully kiss his mom good-bye—which simply provoked further humiliation.

But there was more ridicule for Luke in the Commons, a cafeteria and assembly area where students gathered before starting class each day. The so-called "cools" stood while the outsiders sat. Social standing was considered riding on the answer.

Luke just slumped in a corner, pretended to flick through an exercise book, and counted the seconds until the class bell sounded. Virtually no one even bothered to give him a second glance apart from the jocks, who'd accidentally on purpose bump into him with a heavy thud and not even bother saying sorry.

The only time anyone can remember Luke Woodham hitting back was when one classroom joker tried to imply Luke had a "weird" relationship with his mother because she kissed him good-bye on the cheek each morning when she dropped him off outside school. Woodham exploded with rage at the boy and had to be physically dragged off the other teen.

"Luke went completely crazy. We never saw him like that before and I tell you that other kid would have been seriously injured if we hadn't all pulled Luke away," recalled former classmate Ben Timberlake.

It wasn't long before the solitude and loneliness of being picked on and bullied at Pearl High drove Luke Woodham toward the school library to find his escape from the maddening world. He began reading anything he could lay his hands on. Philosophers like Nietzsche, Aristotle, and Plato; and classical writers like Dostoyevsky and Shakespeare. Soon classmates were ribbing him because he was always buried in a book. The gap between Luke Woodham and the real world was beginning to widen.

Within weeks, Pearl High School had turned Luke Woodham into the classroom misfit. He was the classic loner. Intelligent, introverted, and overweight, and obsessive about his pets and the intense works of many of the most controversial philosophers of the nineteenth and twentieth centuries.

Woodham summed up his feelings at the time, when he wrote in his diaries: "I am not insane! I am angry. People like me are mistreated every day. Throughout my life I was ridiculed. Always beaten, always hated. I am the hatred in every man's heart! I am the epitome of evil! I have no mercy for humanity and became what I am today."

Luke Woodham was already beginning to believe that he was very different from most other kids. All he really wanted was to be his own person, but it seemed that he was being persecuted because he was different. Luke felt that if he didn't fit into a certain clique, then the other kids just made his life a misery.

Everyone seemed to be picking on Luke Woodham. He hadn't made one real friend. Nobody he could truly trust. So he bottled up all his unhappiness and poured all his love and affection into the pets he kept at home.

The concept of Woodham's favorite writer at the time, German philosopher Nietzsche, was that man should be above normal moral codes and go "beyond good and evil." The young, impressionable Luke Woodham was not yet old enough to appreciate what Nietzsche really meant, but he was determined to learn as quickly as possible.

As Woodham later said, "Throughout my life I was ridiculed. Always beaten, always hated. Can you, society, really blame me for what I do?"

Luke Woodham's weight was ballooning rapidly as he escaped from his lonely life with the constant supply of chips and cookies his mother dropped in his school bag every morning. But as he got fatter and fatter, he got increasingly more unhappy and seemed to find it difficult to look most of his high school peers in the eye. Much of the time he shuffled along the school corridors, eyes down in the hope no one would notice him.

And when Luke Woodham did look up, his manic stare simply provoked some of the tougher boys to begin pushing him around all over again.

Luke felt as if he wasn't worthy of anyone's attention. The only students who came near him were the fit, strong sportsmen known to Luke as the "Johnny Footballers," who'd grab his bag of chips or crush his cookies underfoot in the school yard. They all believed he was too shortsighted and too scared to hit back, and most of the time they were right.

But the biggest difference between Luke Woodham

and a child who has a difficult time in school is that Luke was already thinking in terms of getting revenge. Those students would pay for snubbing and ostracizing him. Woodham's growing obsession with philosophers like Nietzsche was already leading him to believe that he could live by his own rules, live by his own laws.

In those early days at Pearl High one of the few students who showed Woodham any compassion was Lea Ann Dew. She lived with her sister Lydia and family a few streets from Luke's house and some mornings would give him a ride into school.

Those rides were very important to Luke Woodham because they meant that he didn't have to get dropped off by his mom, which he knew was seen by other pupils as yet more evidence of his "geekiness."

But Luke Woodham's difficulties in integrating with other students didn't get much sympathy from teachers. They were more concerned with keeping standards at a premium and retaining the school's reputation as one of the finest high schools in the state, if not the entire country.

About the biggest scandal to hit the high school at that time was the occasional bust of kids bringing in a little dope. It was no wonder people from all over the area continued to move to Pearl simply because they wanted their children to attend its high school.

But that reputation was also one of its biggest problems. Many of the new pupils enrolling each school year were the children of new employees of major Pearl businesses, including a cable company, a cardboard box firm, and American Sun Assurance. As a result, long-term friendships often suffered, and there was sometimes a coldness about the way new students were treated.

About the only thing that did impress Luke was the way that all kids of different races and colors were treated equally by teachers and most of the other pupils.

As longtime Pearl Police Department Officer George Burgess later explained: "You don't see what you did back in the seventies when people would sell their homes because a black family moved in next door. That sorta thing just never happened in Pearl. There's a feelin' we're all in this together. Fully integrated."

Throughout Pearl the construction of churches continued at only a slightly slower pace than that of houses.

Five

A short time after starting his freshman year, Luke Woodham made a real effort to change his growing sense of bitterness and rejection. He even wrote a paper on "3 goals for my Freshman year."

In the paper he talked about wanting to pass his exams with "fairly good grades." His second goal was to get along with all his teachers, and his third goal was to start a band.

"I remember Luke trying so hard to act happy and content with his life. He so desperately wanted to do well at school," recalled classmate Jerry Kinder.

Luke's new attempt to integrate himself in Pearl High did have a measure of success because he befriended two teens, Wes Brownell and Daniel Lucas Thompson.

They started hanging out together, but Brownell and Thompson found Luke Woodham quite difficult to understand. Sometimes he seemed like he was from another planet. But all three boys shared a feeling of isolation from the regular crew of students and that helped bond them.

Probably the only time Woodham managed to do anything that would be considered "normal" by most of his peers that year (1995) was to attend the high school prom. The prom had been a subject of much

drama inside the Woodham household because Mary
Anne had effectively barred Luke from going unless
he could get someone to give him a ride to and from
school.

At first, Woodham was distraught because he didn't
know anyone who could provide the transportation.
When Lea Ann Dew, who had been nice enough to
give him rides to high school in the past, heard of his
predicament, she kindly stepped in and agreed to go
with him to the prom.

They weren't dating, but at least Luke got a chance
to go, which probably would not have happened without Lee Ann sweetly volunteering to escort the
younger teen.

The couple even managed a few dances together,
talked, and met other students. It was the one time
Luke had ever felt any warmness toward most of his
peers.

After the prom broke up, Luke and Lea Ann
headed off to eat at Shoney's, but the place was
packed with other students so they ate at a nearby
Waffle House.

But it was only a passing phase for Luke Woodham.
He soon returned to his manic, isolated feelings.

Around this time during the 1995–1996 school year,
Luke Woodham wrote a school exercise about a fictional episode of madness in which he killed teachers,
tortured principals, and looted bank accounts.

The entries were written in poor handwriting, a subject that Woodham dealt with at the start of the document.

"I need to learn to write better. I can only write

good when I write very slow or very fast but my hand gets tired when I write very fast," says the very first entry.

Luke's problem was a classic one. Some days his brain was so overactive, so filled with ideas that his handwriting literally couldn't keep up with what was coming out of his mind.

The thirty-two-page journal assigned for a freshman English class started off like that of a typical teenager bemoaning being grounded by his mom, stating his hopes for passing ninth grade, and writing of his dreams to become a rock star.

Then Woodham, just fourteen at the time, revealed how much he hated himself and his wish to die. This was followed with his secret dream of ruling Pearl and of how he prided himself on annoying his teacher Valerie Neal.

One excerpt read:

If I could spend a day as Mrs. Neal, I would be very very nice to Luke Woodham and pass him for the year. Then I would knock the crud out of the "omniscient dork" for putting junk on my computer.

Then I would go crazy and kill all of the other teachers. Then I would slowly and very painfully torture all of the principals to death.

Then I would withdraw all of my money in the bank and give it to Luke Woodham. Then, I would get all of the other teachers' and principals bank account numbers, withdraw all of the money and give it to Luke Woodham.

Then I would do acid. Then I would get a gun

and blow my brains out all over the dog-gone room and leave my house to Luke Woodham.

In another journal entry, Woodham was assigned to write about an incident that upset his parents. He decided to "write a piece of fiction."
It read:

> I've never really done anything that bad, so I'll make up a story.
> One day I killed a guy and shot his dog in the butt with a big friggin pellet gun. Then, I went to a phone booth and robbed it by yanking the little coin box out of it.
> Then I threw water balloons at some nuns, and I went inside their church and set the priest's wig on fire. (It was the first time I'd heard a good Catholic person say G.D.).
> Then I burned the church down, then, danced around it and sung 2 Nine Inch Nails songs, one called "heresy" and another called "terrible lie."
> Then I robbed a bank and set it on fire. I love to set things on fire, and killed all the tellers. When the police came I killed them all and when the National Guard came, I killed most of them but they finally caught me.

The only students mentioned were his acquaintances Wes Brownell and Daniel Lucas Thompson. He also mentioned Lea Ann Dew.
Woodham fantasized that both teens were part of his rock band, at one point known as the "Residential Slurs."
"The best thing so far about 1995 is the time me

and some of my friends got together and recorded an album," Woodham wrote.

But the inner torment continued for Luke Woodham.

Teacher Valerie Neal took little notice of Woodham's twisted fantasies and the journal's existence did not become widely known until more than a year later.

For whatever reason, the homicidal rantings of Luke Woodham were not deemed serious enough to be of any great threat to Pearl High School. Yet journal entries in the past had been seen as a possible "red flag" that teachers and administrators needed to take seriously. But still nothing was done.

In the mind of Luke Woodham he was throwing dice that said he might or might not do it—it was up to the powers that be to decide.

Most teachers at the time were not trained to identify emotional or psychological defects in a student just based on the writings he or she had submitted. The teachers considered such journals to be an emotional outlet and with large classes throughout Pearl High, it was virtually impossible to focus on the rantings of one kid.

In February 1996, an item on the TV news caught the attention of Luke Woodham, and many of his classmates. Barry Loukaitis, fourteen, had marched into his high school in Moses Lake, Washington, and killed a teacher and two students.

Loukaitis's anger became clear when investigators uncovered the teen's journal. It contained disturbing entries and classmates said he frequently talked to them about killing somebody. Loukaitis was described as quiet, intelligent, and not socially skilled. It sounded a lot like Luke Woodham.

At Pearl High School they called him ugly and fat. He was useless at sports and sank into bouts of lonely depression. Other pupils still teased and bullied him, especially the "Johnny Footballers."

Woodham began thinking about suicide. Every day Luke woke up it became more and more difficult to face the outside world. He went absent from school, but his mom would find out and they would have huge arguments, which would nearly always end with Luke being sent to his room and grounded.

But being grounded didn't mean much to Luke. He rarely went out because he had hardly any friends. Sitting in his bedroom festering didn't help his emotional state by any means. He needed an outlet, but there was nothing.

Locked in that room, surrounded by posters emblazoned with headlines referring to death and destruction, Luke Woodham would escape to another imaginary world where all his problems no longer existed. He later said he looked on the years of 1993, 1994, and 1995 as the most miserable of his young life.

"I was about the only person in my house. And when my mom was there, she, she just screamed and fussed and hollered. I mean, she always talked down to me, and—and she never, never loved me," he later claimed.

Being talked down to was something that really incensed the young and impressionable Luke Woodham. When anyone did that to him it made him seethe with hatred. But, as he later recalled, something inside him kept telling him to continue to keep going. And that was when Christina Menefee entered his life.

* * *

Christina "Christy" Menefee had moved with her family to Pearl in the summer of 1996. She, like Luke Woodham, knew all about the roller-coaster ride of family heartbreak. Her mom, Sheila, and dad, Bob, had divorced ten years earlier and she'd gone to live with her mom.

After six years in the town of Prairieville, Louisiana, just outside Baton Rouge, Christy had a huge bust-up with her mom's new husband, Billy Jeffers. She then joined her father and stepmother, Annette Menefee, in Jacksonville, Florida.

"I married a man she didn't like," Sheila later admitted. "She always loved her daddy. Her daddy always loved her. She just wanted to live with her daddy."

Christy Menefee had dreams just like any young person. She had seriously thought about becoming a veterinarian once, then balked when she learned part of the job was putting down a pet that couldn't be saved.

Christy certainly loved animals. Her white terrier, Fluffy, would follow her through the Menefee house constantly. She also had a hamster called Joey, and a dwarf rabbit called Snow. As a youngster she was also hooked on the cartoon character, the Tasmanian Devil. Even at fifteen, she still lovingly cared for a rose garden in the backyard of the family home.

In the summer of 1996, Christy, her father, and his new family moved to Pearl from Florida. Bob Menefee, not long out of the U.S. Navy and now working as an electrician, had gotten a new job in Pearl, and he'd heard it was one of the safest communities in the South. Bob had even promised to give Christy his 1985 Toyota Camry for her birthday after next—her 17th.

* * *

Christy Menefee arrived at Pearl High School in 1996 not knowing a soul. So gentle, sensitive, quietly spoken Luke Woodham seemed like a really sweet guy. And they had something special in common—a love of animals. Christy also had her own rose garden at home, which reminded Luke Woodham of his mom.

Luke came along at just the right time. She was flattered by his attentiveness and desperate to make some friends in a strange, new environment. So Christy accepted Luke's invitation for a date. Woodham was overjoyed by her decision. He'd rarely even talked to girls, apart from his mom, throughout most of his life. Now he was about to go out with a pretty dark-haired girl with a warm smile and a lot of style. He couldn't believe his luck.

On their first date together, Woodham was deeply embarrassed because Mary Anne insisted on driving the couple to the movie theater—and was then waiting when they got out after the show. Luke didn't really know how to handle the situation. Christy was bemused. She was considerably more mature than Luke and thought it was "kinda weird" that his mother shadowed them everywhere.

Unfortunately, it was yet another example of Mary Anne Woodham's complete inability to be a normal parent. Her overprotectiveness bordered on the obsessional.

Even more significantly, Luke sensed Christy Menefee's feelings about his mother's overprotectiveness. It seemed to him that his mom was going out of her way to wreck his first-ever serious friendship with a girl.

Christy even told her best friend Brook Mitchke: "He's already getting a little too controlling."

She told Brook that Woodham would "get real mad" at her if she didn't call him at a certain time every day or walk with him to class.

Christy's father hadn't been too concerned when Luke insisted on bringing his mother with him to see his daughter one evening. He thought it was just a quaint old Southern custom.

But it did strike Bob Menefee that there was some animosity between mother and son, "but nothing you could put your finger on."

Once, when Woodham and Christy were sitting together on the Menefee family's loveseat, Mary Anne asked, "Do you think y'all are sitting close enough?"

Luke took Christy's hand and replied through gritted teeth, "We're doing just fine, Mom."

Then he looked furiously at Mary Anne and went bright red.

But the other side to all this was that Luke Woodham was in seventh heaven. He was so delighted he had a girlfriend for the first time that he even wrote a page about Christy in one of his notebooks. It was entitled, "The day something good finally came in the mail," and talked about all his inner happiness about being with Christy.

He couldn't quite believe his luck—and he was attentive to Christy to the point of stifling her. He wanted to know what she did every second of the day, whom she spoke to at school, whom she called on the phone.

Luke Woodham was so emotionally immature at the time that he didn't know any other way to behave. He was also massively insecure, so he didn't want any outside influences to put her off him. Luke was used to people laughing behind his back at him, but he desperately didn't want anyone humiliating him in front of Christy—or others telling her bad things about him.

Back at home, Mary Anne Woodham was still trying to stay in control of her son. Not only did she take Luke everywhere in her car, but she insisted on telling him how to wash so he didn't smell bad for his new girlfriend. She tried to get Luke to cut his hair, but he insisted that Christy liked his new, longer style. Luke wanted to tell his mom where to get off, but he didn't want to upset her. He wished his mom would butt out and mind her own business, but in some ways he was joined at the hip to Mary Anne.

Luke couldn't drive and she insisted on taking him everywhere because she thought that even the peaceful streets of Pearl were awash with evil criminals ready and waiting to pounce on an innocent, naive, geeky teenage boy. Although still underage, Luke even meekly suggested to his mom that he be allowed to borrow her car. Besides the need for transportation, he desperately wanted somewhere private for him and Christy to maybe even kiss properly. Up until that point, he had managed nothing more than a brief, shy kiss on the cheek with the supposed girl of his dreams.

Within a handful of dates and a period of less than a month, Christy Menefee knew that although Luke was a sweet kid, she could do a lot better. Some of her brand-new friends at Pearl High also had been pointing out what Christy had suspected from day one: Luke was a weird, slightly slow-witted, fat kid who was an embarrassment to be seen out with.

She decided it would be better to end the relationship quickly rather than break his heart by making him believe it was something more serious than it really was.

On October 1, 1996, Christina Menefee told Luke Woodham that their brief relationship was over. She couldn't handle his bouts of severe intensity and she told Luke she thought she deserved better. She wanted them to remain good friends, but any heavier involvement would be out of the question. Christy also mentioned how embarrassing it was to have a guy's mom out on a date with them both.

Luke was astonished. He'd thought they were only just getting going and that was why he'd only kissed her on the cheek so far. He didn't want to hurry things in case Christy got upset. Now here she was telling him that it was all over. Luke was devastated. He'd seen his whole life mapped out in front of him and Christy had become a permanent part of it.

Luke very quickly started looking around for scapegoats, people to blame for the premature end of his relationship with Christy Menefee. He came up with an obvious target. Luke Woodham had no doubt his mother caused the breakup of the relationship that never really was a relationship. He decided he wanted nothing more to do with Mary Anne. She could go to hell for all he cared. From now on, he'd lock himself in his room and never come out except when she wasn't around.

Luke Woodham was heartbroken. Christina had been his only escape route from the boredom and unhappiness of life at home. He was completely unable to cope with her rejection. He had no one to ask where he'd gone wrong. All he could do was continue to blame his mom.

In his diary he wrote a song that repeated the word

"incarcerated" over and over again because that was how Luke Woodham felt after being dumped by Christy Menefee. He incarcerated himself in his bedroom. The song summed up his roller-coaster emotions when he wrote, "You were all I dreamt of," before the threatening, "You were shit."

Another song that seemed to be aimed at Christy and her decision to end their friendship was called "Dying For You," which summed up what Luke felt prepared to do if he couldn't win back her love.

Christy Menefee didn't help things by sending Luke Woodham a letter in which she said she loved someone else. She also enclosed a photo of herself, which simply confused the emotionally immature boy.

The letter seemed to give him hope with one hand and a slap in the face with the other. It was all perfectly summed up by this brief poem:

Our love is like suicide
Our love is like the pain inside
Our love is like suicide
Our love keeps me alive

"Suicide" was the key word in the poem because Luke was heading straight for a nervous breakdown about his doomed relationship with Christy Menefee. He wanted her to understand just how heartbroken he really was. He decided that sooner or later he would do something that would make her realize it.

Christy Menefee considered Luke Woodham to be something of a pest in the weeks and months following the ending of their relationship. At school, he'd pop up near her all the time. In the commons area, he'd lean against a pillar and just stare across at her without saying a word, a glum expression on his face. His eyes were glazed with sadness.

Luke Woodham felt that throughout his life he'd been an outcast, alone in a cruel world filled with bullies and arrogance. Now he was back where he started.

Six

Luke Woodham's failed relationship with Christy Menefee clearly broke his heart. As he later openly claimed: "I fell in love with her." Woodham had dated Christy for just a few weeks, but it was, in his eyes, the most significant relationship he had ever had.

After the split, Luke was so devastated that he tried to kill himself with one of his father's old guns from his collection on two occasions. He later claimed he was talked out of the suicide attempts by phone calls from Christy and another friend named Jack. Both had called him from school after he'd told Menefee's friends about his plans to die. No shots were ever fired and it's not even clear if Woodham actually took any of the weapons down from the attic of the family home.

Woodham later claimed to school acquaintances he and Christy tried to get back together, but things were never the same after his suicide attempts. Menefee told friends a different story: Their relationship had lasted only a couple of dates before she ended it. However, Christy had noticed how badly he'd taken the split and was genuinely worried that he might still do something stupid.

The worst thing for Woodham was that some months after the breakup, he later claimed, Christy Menefee started taunting him about her involvement with other boys. It was at that time, Woodham revealed, that he began to hate God and started actively trying to find someone he could truly look up to.

Having known Luke Woodham for three or four years, Lucas Thompson considered him a reasonable friend, even though Luke has since said in his journals and diaries how lonely he was.

Thompson found that Woodham continually moaned about how his mother was always either verbally abusive to him or ignored him totally. Thompson did sometimes find the atmosphere at the Woodham house a little heavy to handle when Mary Anne was around. It seemed that Luke and his mother were forever squabbling, fussing, and hollering at each other.

Yet, to Lucas Thompson, Mary Anne Woodham seemed a caring mom most of the time, although she did go out on occasions and leave Luke at home alone. Apart from that, Luke seemed to have a fairly normal family life.

But Luke desperately felt the need to fit in with some group of students—anyone.

Back at school, Luke Woodham, the lonely geek with the Coke-bottle-bottom glasses and baggy cords, noted that many of his classmates were getting heavily involved in role-playing games. It seemed a great way to be friends with other people, but they had to invite you into their game first and no one was likely to ask Luke.

Role-playing games involve a group of players gathered in a room to create or select characters. The most common game at Pearl High was "Dungeons and Dragons." The gamemaster is the person in control of the entire universe, but individuals have free will. The gamemaster is allowed to use predesignated role-playing narrative as an outline for the story and he develops a story line that the other characters follow. The players confront plot twists, political intrigue, and danger as their characters move through the imaginary drama. Players roll dice to determine their characters' response to plot developments.

Luke Woodham was intrigued by the concept of role-playing because it allowed him to be somebody else. It meant he could escape the drudgery of normality by taking on the character of a dark and heroic fantasy figure.

At Pearl High, the gamemaster was often an older student. One of the most popular at the time was Grant Boyette, a senior who was two years older than Luke Woodham.

Boyette seemed to be everything that Woodham was not. His family was deeply spiritual. His father, Marshall, worked in computers and his mother, Lark, was an elementary school teacher in Pearl. They were both founding members of one of the local Baptist churches.

Boyette often wore a dress shirt and tie to school, explaining to friends it was the "Christian" way to dress. His high self-esteem was obvious, and he kept his black hair well trimmed. His neat, sharp facial features automatically made him give off the aura of being in charge, of being smarter than most, of being more cunning, too.

"Grant always looked kinda foxy. He'd squint his

eyes at you if he didn't agree with what you said and then you'd feel him drilling into your mind, trying to work out where you were coming from," explained one former classmate.

Fellow student Lea Ann Dew frequently saw Grant Boyette and his then best friend Rick Brown walk into the cafeteria, which would then fall completely silent while the two teens prayed. Boyette and Brown would always sit at the end of a table, during which time Brown would mumble, "Praise God" and then everyone in the room would go back to eating. Even in a Bible Belt city like Pearl, such devotion during lunchtime was considered unusual, to say the least.

Boyette's Sunday school teacher at the nearby Crossgates Baptist Church was given exactly the impression Boyette wanted his family and teachers to believe.

"What I saw was a kid very smart, very shy, very obedient," recalled Billy Baker. "More of a follower than a leader."

One of the first teens to play role-playing games with Grant Boyette was fellow Pearl High student Jason Pollan. Pollan first met Boyette in the school's Commons area and they soon found they shared an appreciation of *Star Wars*.

Boyette, Pollan, and another friend began a game based on their collective imaginations.

"At that time, the typical story would be that Darth Vadar was a bad guy and by the end of the third movie he's turned into a good guy," said Pollan.

Pollan was the gamemaster who controlled the fictional story line. His own characters would always start off as bad guys, then go over to the good side.

"Basically it's good versus evil and good wins," Pollan later explained. "Grant came over and played in my game, but he became a different person. Some people act out their fantasies, but with him it went overboard real fast."

Pollan quickly realized that Grant Boyette was obsessed with evil for evil's sake. He wasn't interested in ever being a good guy.

Boyette named his role-playing character at that time after legendary revolutionary Che Guevara and his imaginary starship after the former Panamanian strongman Manuel Noriega.

Pollan never forgot the names because most kids would "give their ships names like *Flare* or *Independence.*"

For the following few months, Jason Pollan tried unsuccessfully to weave the game's narrative in such a way that it would lead Boyette over to the good side. Boyette began to introduce ever more evil characters, ones he admired from movies such as *Broken Arrow*, *Virtuosity*, and *Demolition Man*.

Pollan also noticed that while most kids would walk around and interact with other characters that he, the gamemaster, had created, Boyette simply went up to them and shot them for no apparent reason. In cold blood.

"It was lunatic and it got annoying real fast," Pollan recalled.

In a final bid to pull Boyette over to the good side, Pollan invented an evil character called "Kefka." Pollan intended Kefka to be so bad, Boyette could then see how wrong it was to always be the bad guy. But Boyette totally ignored Pollan's efforts and followed the evil Kefka on every move. Eventually Kefka became the leader of the "Kroth"—the group, as Boyette used to call it.

As invented by Jason Pollan, the Kroth were two aristocratic children who had money and power. But once Boyette started manipulating them, the Kroth began to study only the dark side of life.

Pollan recalled, "And after that they learned all these neat illusion powers and how to kill people, the Kroth killed their own parents and took over the planet. Then, once they had control of the main planet, they started a war to take over all the other planets."

In other words, Boyette had created his own, evil version of the game.

The Sunday school character he'd created for consumption inside Pearl High School was nothing more than a mere illusion. The real Grant Boyette couldn't have been more different.

By the time Grant Boyette reached his sophomore year, he openly told friends that if he couldn't be accepted by his peers, then he would seek acceptance elsewhere. He also openly voiced his admiration for Adolf Hitler and admitted to praying to Satan.

"He said he prayed to Satan for power, influence, and money," recalled Rick Brown, Boyette's best friend at the time.

Boyette also told Brown he admired Hitler for the way he could control and manipulate people. He could not have sounded more different from the "shy follower" of people described by his Sunday school teacher.

Shortly after his breakup with Christy, Luke Woodham started working at the Domino's Pizza in Pearl. One of the other Pearl High students working there was Donnie Brooks. The two got to talking one day and Woodham poured out all his fears for the future.

Brooks told Woodham all about a role-playing group headed up by an older Pearl High student called Grant Boyette. Brooks said Boyette was a really cool dude, someone who was not like everyone.

Woodham had already heard about Boyette from Lucas Thompson and Wes Brownell. Woodham liked the sound of Boyette and the two boys decided to try to get into Boyette's group.

In November 1996, Grant Boyette was playing a *Star Wars* role-playing game with Jason Pollan, who soon realized Boyette had remained as obsessed as ever with his characters remaining evil.

Pollan said, "We kept trying and trying and trying with Grant and his character never would go over to the good side. He kept acting evil and eventually it got ridiculous and I knew something was wrong with him. So, as an excuse, I just said I didn't want to play anymore."

That's when Grant Boyette decided to play with younger teens in his own personally molded games. He already had one sixteen-year-old called Justin Sledge on board. Then he heard from Lucas Thompson about Donnie Brooks, Luke Woodham, and Luke's old friend Wes Brownell.

Justin Sledge was a member of Pearl High's Junior Classical League and had studied classics with Luke Woodham. He suffered from lupus, an illness that encompasses various diseases from skin lesions to a chronic inflammation that can involve the joints, kidneys, nervous system, and skin. Sledge's form of the illness compromised his immune system and resulted in the teen having to take regular medication.

Not long afterward, Jason Pollan bumped into Grant Boyette and the teen began regaling him about the games he was running.

"Grant told me some of the things he'd put his characters through," he said. "It was like that's just evil."

Pollan also noted that all of Boyette's games involved characters from the criminal element of society. Grant Boyette seemed to have perverted the goodness of the *Star Wars* characters and turned them into evil incarnate. It truly had become his own personal game.

In November 1996, Pearl High student Troy Parker told his friend Grant Boyette that he was having problems with his mother.

"You just need to go out and kill her," Boyette is alleged to have replied.

Parker couldn't quite believe what he was hearing. He laughed it off at the time, but they all agreed that Boyette's nickname "the Fuhrer" was very apt.

Boyette prided himself on his ability to manipulate others.

Parker was also mildly amused by the way in which Boyette would make a motion like a machine gun when he was pointing out another student to Parker in the commons area of Pearl High School. Boyette would then make the imaginary noise of the weapon. "Bang! Bang! Bang! You're dead, motherfucker!" he'd say and then chuckle to himself.

* * *

Mary Anne Woodham continued her busy round of partying, leaving Luke secluded and alone at home with all sorts of weird thoughts rushing through his mind.

His then favorite quote from his "hero," Nietzsche, on the "Madman" summed up the direction he was heading:

How shall we comfort ourselves, the murderers of all murderers? What was the holiest and mightiest of all that the world has yet owned has bled to death under our knives.

The theory behind Nietzsche's "Madman" was that one day a man would come out in broad daylight, holding a lantern in his hand, going around society saying, "God is dead. We have wiped away the horizon. God had to die because he was the cosmic peeping Tom."

Luke Woodham was all in favor of that particular concept, and increasingly saw himself as that "Madman." His failed relationship with Christy Menefee also continued to haunt him.

"It destroyed me. I couldn't eat. I couldn't sleep. I didn't want to live. It destroyed me," he later admitted.

He still could not come to terms with being rejected by the one and only person in the world he had ever truly loved. This partly explains why he was so pleased to have found some people—Boyette and his group— who wanted to be genuine friends. He desperately needed the company of others.

By December 1996, Woodham and group leader Grant Boyette had already become particularly close compared with the rest of the group, which Boyette was now calling the Kroth.

Luke later explained: "We had a lot of the same interests. We liked to read a lot. We played a *Star Wars* game together. And we would hang out a lot, I guess."

Woodham also liked the way members of the Kroth were considered weirdos by fellow students at Pearl High. It meant they were on a higher plane, according to Woodham.

Boyette was amused by Woodham's ability to make up quotes of great intensity. Among them were: "This country was built on the blood of others, and shall be destroyed in the blood of others," and "God is only a shallow concept made up by fools looking for something to believe in."

Soon after intensifying their relationship in the winter months of 1996, Boyette and Woodham closely studied a book titled *Necronomican*, which had been brought to their attention by Wes Brownell.

Woodham later described it thusly, "It's just a bunch of spells and a bunch of history and stuff like that. Love spells and spells that can kill people and things like that."

Boyette, according to Woodham's later testimony, introduced him to a pentagram, which was like a magic wand with which he could cast evil spells.

Discussing putting spells on people got the teens thinking about all the scores they'd like to settle and how great it would be if they could just wish people they didn't like into having problems—the bigger the better. Luke Woodham grew increasingly fascinated by the entire concept of curses. There were so many people he felt angry and bitter toward.

Lucas Thompson got the distinct impression that

Woodham and Grant Boyette were more intellectual than the others. And because of that, they seemed to live in their own, vastly superior world. It seemed at times to Lucas Thompson to be a world that completely excluded him.

Seven

In December 1996, Troy Parker, an original member of the Kroth, noticed that within a short time of first meeting Luke Woodham, he complained of his terrible home life and how his mom accompanied him on dates and would not let him use the family car.

Parker had linked up with Boyette many years earlier when the two of them, both aficionados of military tactics, talked for hours about weapons and maneuvers, such as placing snipers or hiding a bomb. But the two had eventually drifted apart and Parker was alarmed to see how Boyette and the other members of the group greeted each other with Nazi salutes every morning outside school.

Troy Parker believed that in Luke Woodham, Boyette had found someone weak and impressionable enough to influence in any way he wanted.

By this time Boyette had also proudly proclaimed his group as "the Fourth Reich," although Parker was convinced Boyette had no direct interest in neo-Nazi or skinhead movements. But others who had contact with Boyette at the time really believed the teen's boasts that he carried a handgun at all times, had wads of money, and prayed every day to Satan for even more power, money, and influence.

By the end of 1996, Troy Parker had pulled away from Boyette and his group because, as he explained, "It started seeming serious, and at that same time I was getting old. It all seemed kinda juvenile."

The following month, January 1997, Luke Woodham decided to test out his ability to cast evil spells on a Pearl High student named Danny.

The teen had been over to Woodham's place when another boy, Nathan, had been kicked out of his home and had stayed over at Luke's house. Woodham liked Nathan, but his friend Danny really got on Woodham's nerves.

"He would always talk down to me and he tried to use me any way he could and stuff like that. And I really didn't like it," Woodham said.

One day, Woodham was talking to his new best friend, Grant Boyette, on the phone about the way Danny was treating him. Boyette, according to Woodham's later testimony, told him he would come over to his house and that before he arrived, Woodham was to use the pentagram that he had given him to cast evil spells. The idea was to put a spell on Danny.

Woodham claimed that when Boyette arrived at his house, the two teens also used the *Necronomican,* and Boyette chanted out a spell against Danny.

Woodham later said: "He [Boyette] wanted to just do something to Danny because I told him I didn't want Danny to mess with me anymore. I wanted him to leave me alone."

So, claimed Woodham, Boyette chanted the spell. That was when Woodham saw a picture of one of Danny's teenage friends, Rocky Brewer, in his mind.

* * *

Two nights later, Charles Robert "Rocky" Brewer joined a bunch of high school students at The Park skating rink on Lakeland Drive. A mecca for local kids of all ages, The Park included a putt-putt golf course, the rink, and other activities suitable for all ages.

Brewer left his group of friends after telling them he was going to get a drink on the other side of Lakeland Drive—a four-lane highway referred to locally as the 25.

Two teenage girls driving away from The Park arena on Lakeland Drive noticed the teen cross the westbound lane of traffic, then dash in front of the traffic coming the other way. Suddenly a car heading eastward struck Brewer and sent him flying thirty to forty feet into the air. Less than a minute later, Brewer was found by a group of pedestrians and motorists lying facedown in the grassy area of the shoulder off the highway. He was motionless and twisted and there was blood coming from his head.

The police, called to the scene by the shocked driver of the car, immediately established it as an accidental death.

An hour later, Woodham's friend Nathan turned up at Luke's house, followed a few minutes later by his friend Danny. Danny was in tears and deeply distressed.

"He walked in and told us that Rocky was dead," Woodham later recalled.

Luke Woodham had absolutely no doubt in his mind that Rocky Brewer had died because of the Satanic spell he and Grant Boyette had cast on Brewer's friend Danny.

Woodham later claimed he was so shocked by what had happened that he even asked Boyette about it and the older boy replied: "Well, you wanted Danny to leave you alone; and now he'll never bother you again."

Following the incident, the relationship between Luke Woodham and Grant Boyette further intensified. According to Woodham's later testimony, they started a "proper" Satanic group.

"And," Luke continued, "through the hate I had had in my heart, I used it to try and get vengeance on people and do whatever he [Boyette] told me to do."

Woodham later claimed that the turning point in his belief that demons were invading his world came on the day Rocky Brewer died while crossing the highway in January 1997. The death of the teen reinforced in Woodham's mind that Grant Boyette had the powers to do the things he said he could.

Grant Boyette enjoyed controlling the younger Kroth teens, which included Luke Woodham.

"He basically just told everybody what to do," Woodham recalled. "If there was something that he didn't like, he assigned us all demons."

Woodham had two demons called Mammon, the Persian god of gold, and Dagon, a name that Boyette "gave" to his friend Luke.

Over the course of the next few months, Woodham role-played just about every demon Boyette came up with and there were many.

"Whenever something needed to be taken care of, I would—he would tell me to do it; and I would send them to take care of it," was how Woodham remembered the spells they cast.

He would do just about anything that Grant Boyette

directed him to do. Boyette had the power. He really was the master of the Kroth.

The word "Kroth" is believed to be a bastardized version of the German word *krote*, which means toad. The ancient Egyptians considered the toad to be an animal of the dead because of its preference for dwelling in earth. In the *Herder Symbol Dictionary* under the word "toad," there are pictures of etchings of two toads dancing in honor of Satan. *The Dictionary of Mythology, Folklore and Symbols* shows the toad as both a positive and negative symbol. In Japan, the toad represented an evil goblin whose magical mist "creates beautiful illusions, which lure animals, insects and men to destruction." How much of this was actually known by Grant Boyette and his disciples at the time will probably never be known.

Whenever Grant Boyette started a role-playing game, according to many of his other friends, he would go out of his way to put his characters through hell and back.

"It was like, just evil," Boyette's former gamemaster Justin Pollan later recalled. "While George Lucas's *Star Wars* is a metaphor for real life, all Grant's games had to do with the criminal element of society."

Grant Boyette had twisted the *Star Wars*–style game into his own very personal discipline.

Troy Parker, another friend of Boyette's, stopped playing after a disturbing game at Woodham's house in January 1997. He also said that Boyette got off by always playing the bad characters and then bailing the other game players out of trouble.

That night at Luke Woodham's home, Parker got the distinct impression that Grant Boyette meant every word he was saying. Boyette's role-playing character began boasting about owning his own explosives and automatic weapons. Boyette had mentioned it before, but there was something about the way he said it this time. It was as if he were talking about the real person—Grant Boyette—rather than some imaginary demon.

Luke Woodham was excited and impressed by what Boyette was stating. Some of the others noted it. One of the other members of the group later recalled, "Grant easily controlled Luke because Grant was very intelligent. I'm certain Grant had some kind of power over him."

For Grant Boyette, role-playing was one more tool in his box of manipulative tricks. As the gamemaster, Boyette controlled the entire universe, even though, in theory, individual characters were allowed their own free will. Boyette used a predesigned role-playing narrative as an outline for each story. He then developed a story line, which the characters would follow.

Players were supposed to confront difficult plot twists, political intrigue and danger as their characters moved through the imaginary drama. Grant Boyette's games went on indefinitely until everyone but himself was dead. Boyette and his disciples considered themselves too intellectually superior to play the "Dungeons and Dragons"–style games derived from vampire lore, movies, and comic books.

Boyette always liked to involve at least two of his top six favorite heroes of all time. He announced their biographical details before each game:

ADOLF HITLER (1889–1945)—German dictator who converted his country into a fully militarized society and launched World War II. Hitler—who built the Nazi party and promoted the idea of Aryan superiority—slaughtered millions of Jews and other ethnic groups.

CHE GUEVARA, real name Ernesto Guevara, (1928–1967)—Latin American guerrilla leader who helped Fidel Castro overthrow the Cuban government run by dictator Fulgencio Batista in the late 1950s. Later, Guevara went to South America and led guerrilla armies in an attempt to overthrow the Bolivian government.

MANUEL ANTONIO NORIEGA MORENA (1934–)— Former dictator of Panama, who rose to power with former military strongman Omar Torrijos. A U.S. jury found Noriega guilty of drug trafficking, racketeering and money-laundering.

VIC DEACONS, played by John Travolta, in the movie *Broken Arrow.* Deacons is a renegade Stealth bomber pilot who hijacks nuclear warheads and blackmails the U.S. government.

SIMON PHOENIX, played by Wesley Snipes, in the movie *Demolition Man.* Phoenix, a crazed super-criminal, is revived from suspended animation and threatens the politically correct society of 2032.

SID 6.7, played by Russell Crowe, in the movie *Virtuosity.* Sid 6.7, a computer-generated, police-training villain made up of 180 different serial killers, escapes into the real world and causes havoc.

Outside the core group, Boyette's older friends found it hard to accept that this was the same teen who used to enthusiastically pray to God and attend school meetings of the Christian Fellowship. It was becoming more and more obvious that Boyette's love of role-playing games was becoming a complete obsession.

"Grant loved the manipulative aspects of it. And he clearly preferred playing with the younger kids because they didn't question his ideals," explained one of Boyette's former friends, Todd Carter.

Boyette's old pal Rick Brown immediately recognized the power and influence Boyette had over young Luke Woodham.

"Luke was a social recluse all his life. He [Boyette] thought he would be easy to control and easy to manipulate," Brown later recalled.

Soon after joining the Kroth, Luke Woodham poured his heart out to Grant Boyette about his doomed relationship with Christy Menefee and even mentioned the way she had, in his eyes, taunted him about the other boy she was dating.

Boyette immediately urged Woodham to end the heartache of his separation from Menefee by killing her. She deserved it, Boyette is claimed to have said. The rest of the group was stunned by what they heard. They insisted Boyette told them all what he'd advised Woodham to do.

"He should just kill her and be done with it so he won't have to see her again," Boyette said casually.

Woodham also later claimed that by this time *everything* he did was influenced by Boyette as he strove to gain his acceptance and approval. Woodham believed that Boyette was the only person who truly accepted him for what he was and he felt obliged to constantly show his gratitude.

Meanwhile Boyette reveled in his role as "father" of the group. They continued to call themselves the Kroth, but now Boyette said they had to model themselves on being Satan's Children as well. Boyette even urged the group of teenagers to keep their own notebooks in which they should outline their own special roles, thoughts, and deeds.

Jason Pollan now kept his distance from Boyette because he believed Boyette was a master at the art of manipulation, more than capable of keeping others completely in the dark about his activities.

"He always left the right hand guessing at what the left hand was doing," Pollan said.

Pearl High senior Josh Maxey played in a group similar to Boyette's and he continually resisted the temptation to join Boyette's Kroth.

"When I played, we sat in the room the whole time and we had a friend who would keep records like a notebook or maybe even on computer—and just type the story as it happens or whatever," he explained. "But they seemed to be playing a whole different game."

By the end of December 1996, the group's most regular members were Luke Woodham, Daniel "Lucas" Thompson, sixteen, Donald "Donnie" Brooks II, Wes Brownell, seventeen, and Delbert "Alan" Shaw, seventeen.

Shaw's parents had divorced when he was nine years old and he'd lived with his mother until about a year earlier when his father had been granted custody of him. He'd only just returned to live in Pearl after spending six months with his grandmother in Louisville.

Shaw had a reputation as a mischief maker in the streets near his home in Pearl, even though the only bad habit Shaw himself admitted to was smoking cigarettes. A few months earlier, Shaw made a handful of homemade bombs and blew up at least half a dozen mailboxes near the family's house. It was later believed that Shaw had manufactured his own explosives, made from bomb-making instructions he found on the Internet. Shaw was made to replace all the damaged mailboxes after a neighbor caught him inspecting one mailbox that failed to go off.

Other residents from the houses near the Shaws often spotted the teenager sitting around in the front room of the family house doing nothing but staring manically at the TV set.

One neighbor, Merle Lightsey, tackled Shaw when he called at her house to repay her for one of the blown-up mailboxes. She urged him to do better for himself and get some more sensible hobbies.

"He thanked me for being so nice," Lightsey said. "It was like he never had anybody be nice to him before."

Other neighbors gave Shaw a wide berth after the explosives incident, but one did later insist: "He was just a regular kid, not like some psycho. He never looked like it."

Pearl High senior Lea Ann Dew, who sometimes gave Woodham rides to school in her car, also gave Shaw regular rides to school during the 1996–1997 year. Little was she to know that both he and Luke would allegedly play pivotal roles in a tragedy that would later befall her family.

* * *

Luke Woodham was growing increasingly resentful of his mother. She was always on him because of his grades and he reacted by staying locked in his room playing Marilyn Manson CDs as loudly as possible whenever she was in the house. On the surface, his behavior seemed not much different from a million other teenagers' across the nation.

At home, Woodham read more books, sat in his bedroom strumming his guitar, and began writing poetry. At Pearl High, he continued to be taunted, except when he was with Boyette's group of disciples. Woodham remained convinced that most of his peers simply didn't understand what he was talking about because they were inferior to him.

Grant Boyette and his group had convinced Woodham he should rise above such "vermin."

Perhaps one of the most surprising aspects of life inside the group was that none of their evil thoughts and deeds were fueled by drugs. There is absolutely no evidence of any illicit substances being taken and virtually no alcohol was consumed either.

"In some ways that makes it all the more bizarre. These kids were totally aware of what they were doing," commented one observer.

One night, when Mary Anne Woodham was out partying, Luke crept up into the attic of the house to examine the guns his father had left behind. Luke had considered using one of the guns before when he was contemplating suicide, but this time a Marlin .30–.30

rifle particularly caught his eye, especially when he noticed a box of ammunition near the weapon.

Luke Woodham's world was filled with evil thoughts. His friends in the Kroth would be proud.

Eight

Mary Anne Woodham may have been controlling and domineering, but there is no doubt she really cared about her son. As a former teacher, she was particularly concerned about his education. She'd tried to get more involved in his homework, but she turned it into a strict regime, grounding him if he didn't get the right grades. Whenever Luke fell behind at school, Mary Anne would immediately book an appointment with his teacher.

Mary Anne's attitude undoubtedly alienated her son. The harder she tried to push him, the more he went out of his way to ignore her pressure tactics.

Luke was bright in many ways, but his academic performance was mediocre at the best of times. To make matters worse, he knew that however hard he worked, he could never satisfy his mother.

Food was another part of the same struggle. Mary Anne tried to help Luke lose weight by telling him to stop eating so much, but an hour later she'd give him a pack of chips because he was complaining about being hungry.

Around this time, Luke's friend Wes Brownell began spending more time at Woodham's house after being hurt by a doomed relationship with a girl—similar to Luke's experience with Christy Menefee.

Brownell's best friend, Josh Maxey, later explained, "Wes got depressed, and he just wanted someone to accept him at the time. Basically, he said all they did was go there and watch TV."

Brownell and Woodham spoke in depth about the role-playing games they played with Boyette. It became apparent to Brownell that Luke Woodham was taking Boyette extremely seriously.

Brownell became very worried and tried to warn his friend about getting too involved. But he could tell that Luke felt he knew best—and that he was enjoying himself for the first time in his life.

Anyone entering Luke Woodham's bedroom at that time would have been greeted by a variety of in-your-face homemade posters that some might have found offensive. Luke didn't care.

"America Is Dead" said one. "Fucked Forever" said another.

There was also a home-produced advertisement for the band Luke one day hoped to form.

It read: "Verbal Negligence. If We Cannot Find Life In Order, We Shall Find Death In Chaos. 'One Nation Under My Gun.' "

It's not clear whether Luke Woodham's mother Mary Anne ever bothered to question him about the poster or any part of the manifestos and diaries he'd written over the previous couple of years, but friends later said she was worried about her son's obvious feelings of loneliness and betrayal following the end of her marriage.

Luke Woodham's writings coincided with a period in his life of increasing isolation, an apparent inability to sleep and an obvious state of depression. We will never know if Mary Anne Woodham snooped through her teenage son's diaries and notebooks, but many believe she would have been perfectly within her rights to do so if she was worried about her son's mental state.

Despite Luke Woodham's clear emotional problems, superficially he could function quite well. His character was consistent with having a borderline personality. However, he found it increasingly difficult to be reasonable and make his own independent judgments. His mind was swimming with delusions about his own carefully built fantasies.

Grant Boyette's increasingly regular appearances at the Woodham house could not have been better timed from Luke Woodham's point of view. Boyette and his group remained an ideal antidote to the heartbreak of losing Christy Menefee.

Boyette's own obsession with role-playing games, music, books, and life fed into Woodham's delusional preoccupations, ones that couldn't be further removed from reality.

Woodham later claimed the way Boyette accepted him as a brother made him feel a very special empathy toward the older teen.

By now Boyette and his young disciple were totally locked into casting Satanic spells on people they didn't like. They had convinced themselves that Danny's friend Rocky Brewer really did die as a result of their curse, and that fueled them on to reach for even more real Satanic power.

"There were spells that give you power over the devil

and things to worship the devil with," Woodham later explained. Referring to Boyette, he said: "He put a lot of bad things in my head, and it builds up after time."

Meanwhile, Grant Boyette yet again repeated his claim of owning an AK-47 assault rifle and told his group he had access to many other weapons and a large amount of money, other members later claimed.

Boyette was preparing his disciples for the ultimate rampage of death and destruction. But was it for a role-playing game or for real life?

In February 1997, Luke Woodham got the weekend job as a customer service representative at Domino's Pizza in Pearl. It gave him a chance to get out of the depressing environment at home after his mom had cut off his allowance because, she said, she could no longer afford it.

Within weeks, Domino's area supervisor Glenn Davis found Woodham to be a near-perfect employee. "He always kept to himself. Always been a good worker, always said, 'Yes, sir, no, sir,' got along with his fellow team members."

Woodham even told Davis he was seriously thinking about going into the company's assistant manager's program once he turned eighteen.

The contradictions in Luke Woodham's character would have been obvious to anyone if they'd bothered to look.

Rick Brown, Grant Boyette's best friend from sixth to tenth grade, was increasingly concerned by Boyette's behavior in the first half of 1997.

Brown knew Boyette had joined forces with Woodham and the others to form a game group, but he kept hearing how the teens were getting more and more obsessed with the game. He feared they were all getting in over their heads.

Unlike many others, Brown didn't see Boyette and Woodham as frustrated geniuses always being picked on by their classmates. He regularly saw other students getting a much harder time. And he wasn't very impressed by their choice of reading material, either.

"People see somebody who reads some book on philosophy and think, well, they must be a genius," Brown said. "That's just not true."

Rick Brown had first noticed the beginning of the big change in Boyette's character during the winter of 1996. He had become more vengeful and full of hatred.

"He wanted to prove to the world that he shouldn't have been picked on all his life. That he'd been underestimated," was how Brown put it later.

Brown considered Luke Woodham to be a gentle, harmless kid who he thought was not capable of hurting a fly.

However, "Master" Grant Boyette seemed capable of talking Woodham into doing anything he wanted.

Brown, who harbored genuine ambitions to become a preacher after college, took it upon himself to counsel Woodham in direct defiance of Boyette.

"I spent a lot of time talking to Luke, witnessing to him, and what have you about the Lord and how God could change his life," Brown later recalled.

In fact, Brown reckoned there probably weren't two weeks out of that entire school year that he didn't sit down and talk to Woodham about Christianity.

Brown sensed that Woodham was trying to get away from the influence of Boyette. Others witnessed what seemed to be an emotional tug-of-war between the so-called "devil" Boyette, Woodham in the middle, and "God" in the form of his onetime buddy Rick Brown.

Brown later claimed that on several occasions Woodham went to the First Free Will Baptist Church in Pearl with him and burst into tears.

"He was wanting to get his life right with God," Brown said.

Up until March of 1997, Woodham and Boyette even continued to attend Sunday school at the church. What Rick Brown didn't realize was that Boyette's visits to the house of the Lord were simply intended to prove to his young friend what a sham religion really was.

At the end of March, both Boyette and Woodham stopped visiting the church. It looked as if the devil had already won his biggest battle.

Luke Woodham's treatment at home and by the majority of his classmates had eaten a hole in his soul that was ignited by joining Grant Boyette and his Kroth.

Inside Pearl High, the group was already known as "Satan's Children." They began wearing long black trench coats and most kids went out of their way to avoid them.

"They had a weirdness about them. They seemed to be in a world of their own. Most of us avoided them," remembered one Pearl student.

The best thing about the black trench coats from Luke Woodham's point of view was that it let other students know he was part of a group whom they should not "fuck with," as one of them later put it.

To Woodham, this group of boys represented the first real male friends he'd ever had, or so he thought. Now his life had some purpose. He'd found a way to escape his mother's supposedly harsh treatment of him and the ignorance of his peers.

Luke Woodham and the rest of Satan's Children spent a lot of time discussing and analyzing good and evil. They continued to believe themselves to be above other "normal" people and their morals. Their leader, Master Boyette, encouraged his disciples to ignore "normality" and concentrate on the devil's work. They started to believe they could get away with anything.

One of the group, Wes Brownell, later claimed he did not see any of the rumored occult practices that some of the others claimed occurred inside the Woodham house. Brownell also denied ever reading any of the works of Frederich Nietzche, the German philosopher, whom Luke Woodham so admired.

But Wes Brownell was a much softer person than some of the others in the group. He worked weekends and evenings at the Crossgates Veterinary Clinic in Pearl as a kennel assistant. Brownell specialized in bathing and cleaning up after cats and dogs and was, according to other staff, incredibly loving toward the animals. And despite being involved with the group, Wes Brownell was not considered intellectually superior enough to be involved in the group's innermost activities.

Brownell's best friend, Josh Maxey, later claimed: "Wes told me when he was around at Luke Woodham's they never cast spells or did that voodoo crap or whatever. All they did was sit around and talk about stuff."

Admittedly many of the more outrageous plans were suggested by Woodham but, as he later testified, he felt openly encouraged by Grant Boyette.

They would sit around at the Woodham house, devising all sorts of dark and deathly plans to destroy the world, or whatever. And, said others in the group, they had a bizarre mental comradeship that meant each agreed with the other one's suggestions. And, Woodham claimed, that was when Boyette encouraged him to make his most disturbing decision to date.

PART II

DEATH

"You can't kill me,
I'm already dead."

—Charles Manson

Nine

On Tuesday, April 8, 1997, Luke Woodham decided he didn't want to go into school, and he simply stayed at home. His mother had no say in the matter. She was at work, so she wouldn't find out until it was too late anyway.

Woodham later claimed his friend Grant Boyette joined him at the house and they got to talking about the "beauty of death."

They decided to conduct a morbid experiment: to beat Woodham's once-beloved pet dog Sparkle to see how the animal reacted to excessive pain.

At about four-thirty P.M. that day, Woodham's curious neighbor Merrell Jolly saw the incident. It would have sent shock waves through the area, if anyone had bothered to report it to authorities.

Jolly, who lived one house down from the Woodham residence, watched through the cracks in his fence as the two teens chased the small dog around the backyard, then caught her, and began raining blows down on the innocent animal. Jolly saw Grant Boyette beat the dog with a stick while Woodham held the animal down.

"I could see the dog when he [Woodham] picked it up that it was limp and howling," Jolly would later disclose.

In fact, as Woodham later admitted, in the process of hitting the dog they injured her leg so badly she could barely walk.

That night Jolly told his wife that anybody who'd beat a dog just like that for the sake of it, would end up killing a person. He was referring to Boyette, not Luke Woodham.

Two days later, Woodham's brother, John, noticed Sparkle was limping badly and suggested that his kid brother should take the dog to the local vet. Luke talked him out of it by saying the animal had probably stepped on something and she'd be perfectly fine in a day or two.

Two days after that, on Saturday, April 12, Woodham's older brother once again mentioned the vet, but said he didn't have time to take the dog that day and asked if Luke would do it early the following week.

Woodham later claimed he got scared that the vet would notice the bruises on the animal's legs and he'd get into trouble, so he called Grant Boyette, who arrived at the Woodham house at two P.M.

The two teens then beat the dog even further, and tied her up in a plastic garbage bag, which they then put into two more garbage bags. By now Sparkle was whimpering with pain. They put the garbage bags in an old book bag and set off toward some woods half a mile west of the Woodham residence.

When they got far enough away from the house, Woodham later claimed in one of his manifestos, he took out a billy club he had been carrying and handed it to his accomplice, Boyette. Boyette then took a run at the bag and viciously swung the billy club and crashed it down on the dog.

"I'll never forget the howl she made," wrote Woodham in his manifesto. "It sounded almost human. We laughed and hit her more."

Then Woodham picked up the book bag, now soaked in the dog's urine, and dragged it across the ground deeper into the woods.

A few minutes later, they opened the book bag, tore a hole in the garbage bags, and brought out the top half of the limp animal. They encouraged a bed of ants to swarm all over the once-beloved pet dog before completely removing the limp dog from the garbage bags. They placed her in the book bag, pushing the plastic bags to one side to be burned later.

The two teens picked up the book bag and walked even farther into the woods to a clearing where Woodham pulled out his lighter and some lighter fluid. He made a trail with the fluid across the grass and into the book bag. Then he lit it.

The bag burned, but not quickly enough, so Woodham sprinkled more lighter fluid on the bag, and then they heard the dog scream as the flames licked her body.

Suddenly a hole developed in the bag and the dog stuck her head out. It was completely engulfed in flames.

Woodham sprayed more and more lighter fluid on the animal and the flames continued to roast the dog, scorching and then cooking her skin, but somehow the dog still remained alive.

Woodham claimed in his manifesto that Sparkle managed to get out of the bag at that point, so he took the billy club and hit her on the shoulder, spine, and neck.

"I'll never forget the sound of her breaking under my might," he wrote.

Then they set her on fire again. At one point, the dog opened her mouth and Woodham squirted more lighter fluid down her throat.

Eventually her entire neck and body caught fire, inside and out. When the flames eventually died down, all they could hear was the animal making a gurgling noise. Woodham silenced her for the final time with another smash of the club.

"I hit her so hard I knocked the fur off her neck. I hit her so hard she started to shit," he later wrote. "Then we put her in the burned bag and chunked [sic] her in a nearby pond. We watched the bag sink. It was true beauty."

The killing of Sparkle was a turning point in the life of Luke Woodham. Despite loving that pet dog for so many years, he had suspended his own judgment because he wanted to feel all-powerful for the first time in his life. He also wanted to impress Grant Boyette.

Boyette was feeding on Woodham's insecurities and filling the younger boy's mind with thoughts and deeds that he was incapable of judging. Luke Woodham had in many ways completely lost the ability to make sound judgments about the difference between right and wrong.

Woodham remembered the killing in his manifesto: "On Saturday of last week, I made my first kill. The victim was a loved one. My dear dog Sparkle. Me and my accomplice had been beating the bitch a while . . . we put the subdued little bitch in an old book bag and went to some woods. When we got out to the woods

I took a billy club that I had and handed it to my accomplice." Woodham wrote, "I'll never forget the howl she made, it sounded almost human, we laughed and hit her more. . . ."

(Woodham later claimed that his account in his notes was inaccurate because Grant Boyette told him to write that he killed the dog when it was actually Boyette who dealt the final blow.)

If the two teens could stand witnessing the suffering of an animal, then it wasn't such a big leap to move onto targeting humans.

In some ways, Boyette's alleged control over Woodham was beginning to resemble that of Charles Manson's of his disciples. Some of the similarities were chilling. Manson was a master at allowing his disciples to engage in activities they probably would not have thought of doing on their own. It looked as if Grant Boyette was providing Luke Woodham with the same kind of reinforcement and caring—something so lacking at home.

The killing of Sparkle was also something the teens chose to do together to show that they were leaders of the group.

The slaying of the animal desensitized Woodham. It became a prelude to what he wanted to do to certain human beings. It encouraged him not to shrink away from the ultimate crime he so badly wanted to commit. The urge to kill was growing by the day inside Luke Woodham's soul.

Boyette and his group had all come a long way from when they'd first gathered together. Then, they'd just sat around and discussed the world saying things like,

"Those people who don't like us and appreciate us, there's something wrong with them. We've got the right view, they've got the wrong view."

But by the spring of 1997, Boyette and his disciples firmly believed they had been mistreated, disrespected, put upon, taunted, and ultimately excluded.

Woodham and his teenage friends in the Kroth considered themselves social outcasts, whose anger with society reflected the frustrations of an entire generation. However, the most frightening aspect of the group was the way in which Master Boyette was using all his power and influence to move his members away from what would be considered normal and decent behavior.

The teens were all, in some ways, socially marginal people. They didn't have any other groups to belong to except this one. As a result they were growing in power every day.

The time was approaching to hit back—hard.

The "mystery" of Sparkle's disappearance should have been an event that sparked cause for concern. But Mary Anne Woodham was so preoccupied with work and going out with a succession of boyfriends that the dog's absence was hardly noted until a few weeks after the pet was so cruelly slain.

Luke claimed the animal must have just run away. His older brother thought something was suspicious, but since he was now working long hours as a truck driver, he didn't get that involved with anything in the family home. On one or two occasions John tried to talk to his kid brother about Sparkle's so-called disappearance, but in the end he simply dropped the subject.

Ten

It was in the early summer months of 1997 that Luke Woodham started seeing demons, he later claimed. They were red cloaked with glowing eyes, tall, slumped over, with spikes on their heads, and no hair. But some were different and looked like angels.

Woodham insisted the demons always came to see him at night when he was alone in his bedroom—and they'd only stay for a few minutes.

He said they would tell him things that they wanted him to do, which was to kill people. They put to him the same sort of requests that Grant Boyette regularly did when they got together. It seemed to Woodham that these demons were a simple extension of Grant Boyette. And, Woodham recalled, Boyette always told him when to expect the demons to visit.

While some people later didn't believe Woodham's claims to have met demons, others remain convinced to this day that what Woodham saw he thought to be real. At that time, Woodham was in a state of mind from which any event that supported his fantasies took on real significance.

Luke Woodham had become, thanks to many factors in his life, an angry young man, resentful of many around him. He was prone to serious acting out and becoming overly emotional when he didn't get his own way. Sometimes, he'd lose control and lash out at people.

Interpersonal relationships—apart from Boyette and the group—were virtually impossible for him to form. Woodham could vacillate between being clingy—as he was to Christy Menefee and Boyette—to being distrustful and suspicious of other people's motives.

Woodham was actually starting to believe that he was evil and bad and deserved punishment for being himself. He was convinced that other people didn't like him, or understand him, or care about him. He felt as if he had no one to rely upon apart from Boyette.

"Luke Woodham was a prime candidate for mass manipulation by others. He was seriously disturbed and he had a big problem seeing the world the same way as most people," said psychiatric specialist Mick Jepson, who later examined him. "But most significantly, Luke Woodham at sixteen years of age was cautious and careful in a way most teenagers of his age were not. Usually by that age a person knows their own mind—Woodham clearly did not."

Luke Woodham believed he was lost in a hostile world. It was a world to which he did not belong. One of his favorite means of escape was to sit alone in his bedroom miming out his favorite rock 'n' roll songs on his guitar, imagining he was a famous rock star with that very same world at his feet. When he got to the climax of every song, he, Luke Woodham, believed he was the superstar.

Although Woodham may not have realized it at the time, he was avoiding situations that were emotionally charged because he had less control of his emotions than most sixteen-year-olds.

His tactics of withdrawal, internalization, and concealment had become true assets in his eyes. They allowed him to control himself and rise above the masses.

Luke was, according to later testimony, suffering from classic symptoms of paranoia and what psychologists call psychopathic deviance. He was already on course to becoming a menace to society.

Around this time, Luke Woodham tried to date another girl at Pearl High. Whether it was an attempt by him to escape the clutches of Satan, no one will never truly know.

The girl, a quietly spoken and talented musician, found it very difficult to handle Woodham's romantic overtures.

Luke was eventually rejected by the girl and made to feel even more inadequate when she told him she wouldn't go on a date with him "even if he were the last boy on earth."

"She just didn't realize how messed up Luke was at that time. If she'd realized, I'm sure she wouldn't have cut him down so cruelly," said one person, who later spoke to the girl.

Being rejected by another girl further fueled Luke Woodham's hatred of his peers and pushed him further into the clutches of Satan's Children, and Grant Boyette.

Shortly afterward, Christy Menefee told a couple of her closest friends that "geeky" Luke Woodham was once again pestering her for a date. She told friends it was nothing more than a harmless crush on his part and she had no intention of dating Luke again.

But Christy Menefee was irritated by the way Luke

had started stalking her around the school again. She tried to play it cool and her friends said she wasn't worried by Woodham's almost psychotic behavior.

Her friend April Evans later recalled: "I never heard them talking or fighting or anything. It was kind of like, 'He was my boyfriend. Who needs him?' "

Luke Woodham's failed attempt to make another date with Christy made him feel he was humiliating himself. His love for her had turned to hatred because of the way she brushed him off by implying she had other fish to fry.

Christy told another former boyfriend that Woodham had been stalking her that early summer of 1997, but again, she sounded very unconcerned. Christy thought she could more than look after herself. She was a hardy, energetic young lady and very proud to be a junior ROTC member at Pearl High.

Junior ROTC naval science instructor Charles Sandler had been so impressed by Christy Menefee, he had taken her on a course at the SeaBee Base in Gulfport just a couple of months earlier.

Meanwhile, all Luke Woodham wanted was to be in her company and feel as if he was like everyone else. For all his bravado talk with Boyette and the rest of the group, Luke Woodham longed to be "normal" in many ways. But he knew in his heart of hearts it would never really happen. And when that realization dawned on him, Luke Woodham got madder than ever before.

How dare she make a fool of him?

How dare she tell her friends what a geek he was?

How dare she reject him?

Woodham was growing bitter and twisted. His mind was filling with evil thoughts and deeds.

* * *

A couple of weeks later, Christy Menefee's close friend April Evans overheard a chilling encounter between Woodham and the object of his obsessional desire.

"I heard him threaten to 'put a bullet' in her head a couple of times," Evans said.

When she asked Christy Menefee if she was scared about Woodham's threats, she brushed it off—just like most of the students at Pearl High, no one took Luke seriously.

Christy Menefee had a big future ahead of her and minor irritations like Luke Woodham wouldn't get in her way.

In the early summer of 1997, Luke Woodham was feeling so confused by Christy Menefee's continual rejection that he wrote in his diaries: "No one truly loved me. No one ever truly cared about me. I only loved one thing in my whole life and that was Christina Menefee."

Christy's rejection of Woodham pushed him further and further into Satan's Children. He was convinced he would never be able to have a relationship with a normal person.

Grant Boyette grew incensed when he heard yet more details of Luke and Christy's doomed relationship from Woodham. He once again urged the younger teen to take revenge, just like they had with that irritating Pearl High student Danny. Boyette even made Luke his self-proclaimed, role-playing "assassin" as if to emphasize the point.

The "master" Boyette had a lot of jobs in the pipeline for his young "assassin."

* * *

In May 1997, Wes Brownell was so freaked out by the group's obsession with death and destruction that he started to give them all a wide berth, including his friend Luke Woodham. Brownell was so frightened, he started screening the telephone at home and wouldn't return any calls from Woodham.

Brownell told Josh Maxey, "Man, they're getting out of hand with it."

"What d'you mean?" asked Maxey.

"I don't want no part of it," said Brownell.

Maxey never did find out what "it" referred to.

Back home, Mary Anne Woodham continued treating her son Luke as if he were still ten years old. It made him an even more remote figure and he was growing ever more resentful of his mother by the day.

When Luke wasn't with his group of friends, he would lock himself in his bedroom and read his favorite philosophers over and over again. Then he'd listen to his favorite CDs again and again. Then he'd write lines of poetry.

Woodham desperately wanted to make the ultimate impression on Grant Boyette. After all, Grant was his only true friend in the world.

By casting Satanic spells and absorbing the joys of reading books on subjects such as astrophysics, Woodham believed he had been transformed from a student who failed his freshman year to an intelligent human being.

"I felt like I had complete control and power over a lot of things," Woodham said.

Up until this stage in his life, Woodham had been emotionally vulnerable, suffering from a troubled home life, and deeply hurt by his failed romance with Christy Menefee.

Grant Boyette and his group of disciples had changed all that the day Boyette told Woodham, "I worship Satan, and Satan's chosen you to be part of my group."

Boyette even encouraged Woodham by telling him: "You've got the potential to do something great."

Those words were, Woodham later claimed, like music to his ears. They lifted him out of the humdrum doldrums of life into a place where he was someone. He meant something.

Luke Woodham dearly wished the same could be said of his treatment at home. The house was filthy. There was never any real food in the refrigerator. His mother was out most nights.

Woodham's world was getting smaller and smaller. He shuffled through school in a virtual daze. He lived an even more insular existence at home, except when Grant Boyette and his disciples appeared on the scene.

Eleven

Around this time, a network that helped abused and battered women and children and offered counseling for dysfunctional families got an anonymous call from one of the Woodhams' neighbors.

They had heard screaming coming from the house on Barrow Street and there were genuine fears that someone inside the house might be in physical danger.

However, when a member of the Resource Center Network in Pearl called at the house that same day, Mary Anne Woodham came to the front door and insisted there were no problems. The counselor had no choice but to leave the property and no report was ever filed with the police or any other agency.

Boyette and his group of outcasts continued their regular discussions about the destruction of the world and their pivotal role in it. The killing of Sparkle was still fresh in their minds. Some of the group had experimented with explosives. Now they wanted to progress beyond shattering windows and mailboxes, to something that could potentially maim and kill.

Boyette was by this time calling himself "Master of High Demon Activity" and he encouraged every turn of the discussions.

Explosions "expert" Delbert Alan Shaw was given the title of Commander-in-Chief (Explosives) and told to come up with a master plan. Shaw believed he could manufacture his own version of napalm by using Styrofoam and gasoline. He'd even tested it in a ditch deep in the woods one afternoon. Shaw was considered highly experienced thanks to those mailbox bombings in the streets near his home in Pearl.

In the middle of all this talk of subterfuge and raids on the high school, group member Donnie Brooks mentioned to Boyette and Woodham that he was having a lot of problems with his dad, who'd put him on an eight o'clock P.M. curfew. If the curfew was enforced, it would mean Brooks might not be able to attend the group's meetings.

Master Boyette and his assassin, Woodham, were outraged that Donnie's father—a tough-talking Pearl City fireman—would dare put such restrictions on his son. Boyette urged Brooks to lay his feelings about his father completely on the line. He wanted to hear the full story. It emerged that Brooks had stolen one of his father's credit cards and run up a bill of several thousand dollars.

By the end of that meeting, Brooks was being encouraged by Boyette and the others to plan the murder of Brooks's father. Boyette's attitude and approach were not dissimilar from what he'd been saying to Luke Woodham about Christy Menefee.

It seemed that Master Grant Boyette believed that "the enemy" should be exterminated without question. He also mentioned that Brooks might have to find some money to pay out if the killing was successful, Brooks later claimed.

Within days, the group had come up with an extraordinary plot to kill Donald Brooks, Sr. They were going to coat certain doorknobs in the Brookses' house with a special poison acid that, the moment the elder Brooks touched it, would seep into his body and he'd be dead within minutes.

On the face of it, the plan sounded like a farfetched scheme dreamed up by a group of bored teens. But the Kroth were deadly serious about their intentions.

The beauty of it, said Boyette, as he explained the plan to his disciples, was that the poison was virtually untraceable in the body's system and the victim would look as if he'd had a heart attack.

The group seemed very excited by the plan, but Donnie Brooks felt he was being pressured into having his father killed. He'd been annoyed at first about his dad's curfew order, but now, as the dust was settling, he realized that taking the law into your own hands might not be the answer.

At Luke Woodham's messy, dusty house that evening, the group put together detailed plans for murdering the elder Brooks. Donnie tried to tell them not to go ahead. But they didn't seem to want to listen.

Donnie Brooks had already been spooked by Boyette's response when Luke Woodham dared to question his "master" about another issue.

Woodham convinced the other members of the group that the previous night he couldn't get any sleep because one of Boyette's role-playing "generals" was sitting outside Luke's bedroom window. Donnie Brooks believed that incident was yet more evidence of Boyette's threat to use demons to harass any of the group into doing whatever he wanted.

As he later said: "Grant said Luke was a prime target for Grant's demons because he would do whatever

Grant said, and Luke was evil minded. I believed at the time that Grant had that power [to summon demons], and I still believe it."

So when Brooks said he wanted the group to quit their plan to murder his father, and Boyette turned on him saying, "You know too much about the group. You're either with us or you're dead," it sent a chill up Brooks's spine.

Boyette and Woodham then proudly told Donnie Brooks every detail about the death of Sparkle. They wanted to be sure he got the message loud and clear. But all it did was further reinforce Brooks's conviction that he needed to get away from the group as fast as possible.

Donnie Brooks was especially disturbed by the amount of power Boyette seemed to wield over Luke Woodham. Brooks really began to believe that Boyette had the power to make him do anything. He also sensed that Boyette was trying to encourage Woodham to kill his father. He realized he had to pull out of the game before it was too late. But Brooks was understandably fearful about his own safety.

Satan's Children continued discussing their much grander plan: the complete and utter destruction of Pearl High School, the heart of their life at that time. Woodham, who loathed school, was extremely enthusiastic.

The idea that had originated with some childish comments about other students they didn't like had grown into something far more sinister and filled with genuine, evil intent. Grant Boyette is alleged to have urged the others to spill blood in the school with this bizarre, cryptic advice: "Don't split up! By pooling your skills and resources, you can escape the Imperial attack!"

Master Boyette, investigators later alleged, further encouraged his assassin, Woodham, and his friends to plot the takeover of Pearl High School by reinforcing that they should allow five minutes for executions before blowing up the entire school and fleeing to Cuba.

"We cannot move forward until all our enemies are gone," Boyette allegedly told his friends. He again mentioned an AK-47 assault rifle, having access to large sums of cash, and a selection of other deadly weapons.

The only member of the group who seemed one hundred percent behind the high-school-destruction plan was Luke Woodham. This audacious plan for death and destruction started a clock ticking inside his mind.

Now the countdown had begun. The thin line between fantasy and reality had become so blurred for Luke it no longer existed.

Yet there was another side to Luke's character. It was a side that longed for normality—a happy home life, popularity at school.

Around this time, he made yet another effort at writing a song for his imaginary rock 'n' roll band; the lyrics were filled with optimism and referred to such normal pastimes as drinking in bars and having fun.

June 3, 1997, was a "momentous" day for Luke Woodham. In his diary he swore he would never again be put in a position where he could be hurt by a woman.

He signed his entry with his initials in a smudge of his own blood.

The clock inside his mind was ticking away and nothing was going to stop it.

Donnie Brooks was so freaked out by the imminent threat to his father's life that on June 11, 1997, he gave a statement to Rankin County Youth Court in which he claimed there was a plot by a group of teens called the Kroth, led by Grant Boyette, to kill his father.

Brooks even claimed the perpetrators intended to kill his father by placing a fat-soluble poison on a doorknob in the Brookses' family home.

In his statement, Brooks quoted Grant Boyette as saying, "If you are not with me, you are against me. If you are against me, you are dead."

In another portion of his statement, Brooks wrote, "Grant is the leader of the Kroth. He is supposed to have direct contact with Satan and his 'general.' "

Brooks even conceded, "Where I went wrong is I stopped following God. My life had hit an all-time low. Instead of asking God for help or my friends and family for help, I listened to [others] . . . that would be interested in my soul in exchange for money or whatever I wanted. I said no. But things got worse and Satan got me when I wasn't looking."

Brooks also signed a statement admitting he had stolen his father's credit card and run up bills of ten to fifteen thousand dollars for stereo and computer equipment and car parts and accessories.

He further admitted to stealing fifty to seventy-five

dollars from his stepsister to buy things for Grant
Boyette.

It has never been fully established whether the Pearl
Police Department was informed about Donnie
Brooks's "confession."

Chief Bill Slade was undoubtedly proud of his department's record in the community and he was fond
of telling everyone just how well-equipped his officers
were. While Donnie Brooks was trying to warn authorities of an impending disaster, Chief Slade was proudly
unveiling the purchase of a sophisticated radio-and-
telephone system for his officers. To keep police in
touch with the community's biggest menace—speeding
drivers—seventeen new radar guns for patrol cars were
on order.

Donnie Brooks's confession went unheeded. Pearl
authorities couldn't possibly take seriously the plans of
a bunch of school kids.

Twelve

Luke Woodham was bitterly disappointed when Master Grant Boyette announced the cancellation of the assassination of Donald Brooks, Sr. Whether any of them knew that Donnie Brooks had made a statement to authorities is not known to this day. But they certainly suspected that Brooks had informed on them and Boyette made the decision to cancel the bizarre scheme.

Luke saw the cancellation of the Brooks' job as even more reason to step up the plan for the destruction of the high school and certain individual "targets."

This event happened to coincide with his getting yet another rejection from Christy Menefee, who was now growing extremely fed up with dealing with the love-sick teen.

Woodham was so furious that he allowed his hatred for Christy to reignite. His sense of frustration continued building up inside his twisted mind. He needed an outlet with which to channel all his frustration and anger.

The clock was still ticking inside his head, counting down the days and weeks until he committed the biggest atrocity of all.

Woodham and Boyette talked in more detail about the specific people they were going to kill and maim

at Pearl High School. Some of the other members of
Satan's Children were a little more cautious. Understandable, if in their minds it was all still just a game.

Luke Woodham wanted to show he really meant
business. He needed to impress his friends, to gain
their ultimate approval.

Many of the others found it difficult to take the
sixteen-year-old seriously, with his bookish, introverted behavior. Overweight, wearing thick glasses to
compensate for his poor eyesight, was anything Luke
Woodham said worth taking seriously?

At home, Luke Woodham's hatred for his mother
was growing by the day. Every time they had another
argument, he thought how much better life would be
without her. Even their regular pitched battles about
mowing the lawn had turned much more threatening,
with Luke calling Mary Anne every name under the
sun while refusing to help. Woodham saw it all as being
part of a far bigger picture.

"She never loved me," he later said. "She blamed
me for my dad leaving. She blamed me for my brother
hating her. . . . She was always against me."

Like every sixteen-year-old, Luke Woodham felt the
winds of liberty blowing his way. He wanted freedom
to travel outside the home. He saw it around many of
the other members of the group, especially Grant
Boyette, who had become almost like a surrogate father to him.

The problem was that the negative points far out-
weighed the positive and Luke felt absolutely powerless
to extricate himself from the situation. He could have
run away, but he knew he'd never survive. Luke's solution was to crawl even deeper into his own head,

isolating himself from everyone, apart from his beloved group.

Yet despite all his seething hatred of his mother,
Luke remained the dutiful son to Mary Anne. He still
worried about her when she got home drunk from yet
another party.

But in those summer months of 1997, Luke started
to imagine a brighter future. It was a future in which
he even began standing up to his mother.

In early September 1997, Luke Woodham had a minor pushing match with seventeen-year-old junior Kyle
Foster, son of the Pearl mayor, Jimmy Foster.

Foster had a reputation as a tough guy inside the
high school and he was a very highly rated tight end
for the Pearl Pirates football team. To Luke Woodham,
he was a typical "Johnny Footballer" throwing his
weight around by bullying the weak and shy. One day,
thought Woodham to himself, one day he will pay.

Also in early September, Luke claimed Master Grant
Boyette stepped up his pressure on assassin Woodham
to take bloody revenge on Christy Menefee for breaking his heart.

Discussing yet another version of the high school
bombing-and-shooting rampage, it was agreed she
would be one of the victims when they burst into the
school with automatic weapons bristling and grenades
ready to pop.

As Boyette spoke, Luke Woodham could visualize it
all. His eyes glistened with excitement.

"He looked really into it. There was no question of
Luke thinking we were all just playing games. He was
deadly serious," recalled one member of the group.

Woodham later said he was completely under the control of Boyette by this time, although he sensed that Boyette was using his (Woodham's) rejection by Menefee as a means to force him into doing something very drastic.

Boyette's visits to the Woodham house were by now so regular that he didn't knock before entering the front door, which Luke deliberately left unlocked just to irritate Mary Anne.

Woodham claimed he still tried to resist Boyette's pressure. "I tried to let go, but he [Boyette] wouldn't let me drop it."

One day Woodham said he even told Boyette: "I got real doubts about all this, Grant."

"You have to do it," the older teen is alleged to have replied.

Boyette, according to Woodham, then continued: "You are nothing. Gutless. Spineless. Nothing."

Luke Woodham was faced with the choice of losing his only true friend in the world or going through with a deadly game of revenge. He knew which choice he had to make.

On the last weekend of September 1997, Luke Woodham took a phone order at Domino's from Pearl High Assistant Principal Joel Myrick. Woodham considered Myrick a reasonable teacher compared with most he encountered, so he gave him a discount for placing an order for three pizzas.

Myrick thought nothing of Woodham's favor. He barely knew him, but it seemed a pleasant gesture.

On Sunday, September 28, 1997, Master Boyette told assassin Woodham that their murderous plan to get revenge on the world was in its final stages. Woodham reacted by producing a book called *The Satanic Bible* by Anton LaVey. A crucial passage discussing the best time to perform certain actions had captivated Luke Woodham.

LaVey had written that the most effective time to perform a ritual was about five o'clock in the morning, roughly two hours before the person awoke.

Grant Boyette later claimed that he had no intention of taking their so-called plans for a school massacre seriously.

October 1 would be the first anniversary of the breakup of Luke Woodham's ill-fated relationship with Christy Menefee. That date bored a hole in Woodham's psyche. He had to find a way to acknowledge the anniversary that was only one day away. Woodham had been fuming and plotting for long enough. It was time to turn his genocidal fantasy into a reality.

That afternoon, September 30, 1997, neighbor Sherilynn Friend saw her friend Mary Anne Woodham out in the garden of her house on Barrow Street. Mary Anne waved as she looked up from her beloved rose beds.

Sherilynn Friend then noticed Luke Woodham looking out his bedroom window—just staring into space. She had no way of knowing Luke and his mother had just had yet another furious argument over Luke's wanting to borrow Mary Anne's white Corsica. She'd refused because Luke did not even have a full license and, as she was fond of reminding her son over and over again, his eyesight was poor.

Luke was infuriated by his mother's attitude. He had

rushed to his bedroom and slammed the door shut behind him, refusing to come out for the rest of the day.

That evening, group member Lucas Thompson started to get "real worried" about Luke's state of mind. He called him up on the telephone.

"Gonna kill her in the morning," was the first thing Woodham told his friend.

Woodham was whispering to make sure his mom didn't hear. The conversation continued:

"How you gonna do it, Luke?" asked Thompson, according to his own later testimony.

"With a knife," came Woodham's reply.

Woodham at no time blamed anyone else for talking him into committing the murder.

Thompson couldn't believe his friend would go through with it. But then Thompson remembered how Luke had taken an oath of allegiance to Grant Boyette, and he'd heard Boyette referring to demons and curses.

Even Thompson in the past had found himself prepared to do things for Boyette—such was the power of the older teen.

"Sometimes he might ask me to keep an eye on somebody or listen to what they're talking about," Thompson later said.

But surely Boyette would never ask someone to kill, would he?

Luke Woodham had remained cool and calm throughout the conversation.

As Woodham himself later chillingly admitted: "I just stopped caring on Friday for some reason."

Later that same evening, Sherrilynn Friend was out

walking when she noticed Mary Anne getting out of her white Corsica in the driveway.

They exchanged pleasantries. As Friend later recalled: "Just a quick hi and bye." She thought nothing of it until the next morning.

That night, Lucas Thompson became increasingly worried about what he feared Luke Woodham might be capable of doing. Thompson was only too well aware how much Luke had changed since he'd joined forces with Boyette. But could Luke possibly be serious about his intentions?

In Luke Woodham's bedroom was a booklet that came with an introductory *Star Wars* role-playing game. It advised that setting up the game was like writing a good short story. You had to provide an interesting setting and a conflict. The characters had to be given a goal in each adventure.

Luke Woodham had the conflict planned, the setting, and a deadly goal to start putting into action the following morning—the anniversary of his doomed relationship with Christy Menefee.

He wanted the celebration to be something completely unforgettable.

Thirteen

Luke Woodham had a sleepless night, tossing and turning. He later claimed his mind was buzzing with strange visions.

Just before five the next morning, October 1, 1997, his alarm went off. It was time to execute stage one of his master plan to change the world.

The early signs of daylight peeping through the drapes would, according to many of the books Grant and Luke had read, make the demons even more receptive to his actions. Dawn was the best time to strike.

Woodham later insisted that all he could see when he woke up were the demons. "I'd see them whenever Grant had told me to do something," he said.

They were telling Woodham that he was nothing and that he would always be nothing. He would never be anything if he didn't do what he'd set out to do.

Woodham went to the kitchen and took a large hickory knife with a brown handle out of a drawer. Then he headed back to his bedroom and took a pillow from his bed.

He was about to walk out of the room when he noticed his silver aluminum baseball bat. He picked that up as well.

Just as Luke was coming out of his door, he noticed

his mother walking into the kitchen. It surprised him because he thought she'd still be asleep.

He braced himself and followed her.

Less than a minute later a terrified Mary Anne Woodham ran into her bedroom and tried to shut and lock the door, but she wasn't strong enough to hold it closed.

Inside the bedroom an ironing board fell over as Luke forced his way in. He smashed his baseball bat down on a chest of drawers and then swung at a dresser.

Mary Anne cowered on the double bed. She had no place to hide.

Woodham later claimed that was when he heard Boyette's voice again, urging him on.

"He told me I had to do all of this and that I was nothing and that I'd always be nothing, every day that I lived, and that I would never be— I'd never be anything."

Luke then closed his eyes, and: "I just followed myself. I didn't want to do any of it. And I remember I just kept hearing his voice."

He again looked down at his mother crying and pleading, scrunched up on the corner of the bed in her favorite pink jogging pants and sweatshirt.

Luke Woodham took a long, deep breath. He lifted the baseball bat up above his head and held it there for a beat.

Then he crashed the bat across his mother's face with the force of a runaway train. It fractured her jaw. He dropped the bat on the floor. He forced the pillow over her face and switched the hickory knife from his left to his right hand.

He plunged the long blade into her body, wildly stabbing and slashing at her with the knife in one hand, while trying to force the pillow to stay over her face with the other.

Over and over and over again.

Mary Anne Woodham, 5-foot-8, 145 pounds, tried to protect herself by throwing up her arms as her son's attack increased intensity. At one stage she forced the pillow off her face. Her eyes locked on her deranged son and she pleaded for his mercy.

He reacted by forcing the pillow back over her face. During the struggle he even cut himself on his hands with the knife.

Seconds later, she completely surrendered. Mary Anne Woodham had succumbed to injuries that included a crushed jaw, a brain contusion, seven stab wounds, and eleven slashes to her body.

"I remember hearing Grant's voice, saying I'd be nothing," Woodham later claimed. "I remember hearing his voice. My eyes were closed, and when I opened them, my mother was lying in her bed, dead."

Woodham insisted he had not been aware of what he'd done until that moment when he opened his eyes.

"That's it. That's all I know," he said.

The reality is he used not one, but two weapons to extinguish his mother's life. He didn't bother tying her up. He simply crushed and beat the life out of her.

Murder was on Luke Woodham's mind.

And he had more "work" to do.

* * *

Experts are convinced that something else happened that Luke has refused to reveal, either because he consciously refuses to, or because, like so many of his other appalling experiences, he cannot remember.

It seems that perpetrators are frequently deliberately silent about certain events they find overwhelmingly shameful, even when those revelations might help their defense in a court of law.

Perhaps Mary Anne had grounded Luke for something trivial or maybe slapped his face in a fit of temper. Sadly, we will probably never know.

After killing his mother, Luke Woodham walked to the kitchen and tried to treat the cuts he'd gotten on his hands during the frenzied attack. He dabbed alcohol on them and then put a bandage over each hand.

He went back into his bedroom, sat down at his desk, and wrote out a last will and testament quoting his favorite philosopher Nietzsche.

It was, many later remarked, more like a personal manifesto on life and death.

It read:

I, Luke Woodham, being of sound mind and body, will to Grant Boyette my books. To Lucas Thompson: My guitar and amplifier and their equipment . . . I also leave my writings of philosophy and poetry to Grant Boyette. They are parts of me and must be published as pieces of my life. Also, to Grant Boyette, I will all my cassette tapes.

Throughout my life I was ridiculed. Always beaten, always hated. Can you, society, truly blame me for what I do? Yes, you will, the ratings wouldn't be high enough if you didn't, and it wouldn't make good gossip for all the old ladies.

I am the hatred in every man's heart! I am the epitomy [sic] of all evil! I have no mercy for humanity, for they created me, they tortured me until I snapped and became what I am today!

Hate until you can't hate anymore. Then learn, read poetry, books, philosophy books, history books, science books, autobiographies and biographies. Become a sponge for knowledge. Study the philosophy of others and condense the parts you like as your own. Make your own rules. Live by your own laws. For now, truly, you should be at peace with yourself. Live your life in a bold new way. For you, dear friend, are a Superman.

I am not insane. I am angry. This world shit on me for the final time. I am not spoiled or lazy, for murder is not weak and slow-witted. Murder is gutsy and daring.

People like me are mistreated every day. I do this to show society "push us, and we will push back." I suffered all my life. No one ever truly loved me. No one ever truly cared about me.

I only loved one thing in my whole life and that was Christina Menefee. But she was gone a way from me, I tried to save myself with [   ], but she never cared for me.

As it turns out she made fun of me behind my back while we were together. And all throughout my life I was ridiculed. Always beat on, always hated.

Woodham went on to curse Christianity, society, and his lifelong suffering in the five-page document.

> Hate humanity! Hate what humanity has made you! Most of all, hate the accursed god of Christianity . . . fill your heart, mind and soul with hatred until it's all you know.

He ended the manifesto by writing: "Wednesday 1, 1997, shall go down in history as the day I fought back."

When Luke had finished, he got up and left his room. On the bed he left the knife, the aluminum baseball bat, a Marilyn Manson CD, an empty box of .30–.30 rifle shells, shotgun shells, and an empty camouflage rifle sheath.

Assassin Luke Woodham then telephoned Master Grant Boyette to announce he was about to carry out the next stage of Boyette's orders.

Woodham later insisted under oath that he had told the older teen that he'd killed his mother. However, in the middle of the conversation, another member of the group, Lucas Thompson, came on the line and Woodham put Boyette on hold.

"You on the other line with someone?" asked Thompson.

"Yeah, Grant."

Woodham had sounded different from the previous evening—more teary. Thompson took a long gulp, then asked the question that really mattered.

"Have you done it?"

"Yeah, I've done it," came Woodham's reply.

Lucas Thompson suspected that Woodham had killed his mother.

Grant Boyette might have been "the father" to him and other members of the group, but that didn't mean Woodham had to kill his mother just because Grant had said to do it. That was plain crazy, thought Thompson.

Luke Woodham went back on the line with Grant Boyette and spoke to him for a further two minutes.

No one to this day knows what orders Boyette did or did not give to his young disciple, but shortly after Woodham put the phone down, he began the next stage of his "mission" as Grant Boyette's assassin.

Woodham went up to the attic where he grabbed his father's favorite hunting rifle.

It felt surprisingly heavy, but then Luke Woodham had never properly handled a gun before in his life.

At about 6:45 A.M., Sherrilynn Friend had just walked back into the kitchen of her apartment next to the Woodham house when she heard a loud bang. She later recalled it sounded like a door being shut. She remembered the time because she'd just put the garbage out.

Friend looked out of the window in the direction of the Woodham house. Not long after, she heard the squealing of tires and saw Mary Anne's white Corsica moving on the driveway.

Then Sherrilynn Friend noticed it was Luke driving the car. She knew he didn't have a driver's license and he was driving erratically and fast. He swerved to avoid a fence on his way onto the street.

"He just pulled out—like really fast," Friend recalled.

Also watching the white Corsica reverse wildly across

the street almost crashing into the fence was Luke's classmate Kacy Strauss and her mother, Jeanette.

Mrs. Strauss knew immediately something was wrong because Luke didn't drive due to his poor eyesight. Mary Anne Woodham usually took her son to school before going on to work.

But Mrs. Strauss did nothing.

In the car, Luke stroked his dad's old .30–.30 Marlin hunting rifle, reassuringly on the seat beside him.

Fourteen

The Commons in the main Pearl High School building was buzzing with students and teachers from as early as seven-thirty that morning. Many of the teenagers had Bibles in their hands because they'd just been to early morning prayer.

Luke Woodham's friend Wes Brownell walked into the Commons—the large, open indoor hallway surrounded by a cafeteria and administrative offices—at around 7:45 A.M. with his friend Josh Maxey, a senior. As the two youths walked through the area, Christy Menefee approached Brownell.

"I haven't seen Luke in two or three days. Is he okay?" she asked Brownell. "I'm worried about him."

Brownell replied, "I don't know. I haven't spoken to him since May. I don't hang with him anymore."

Brownell then moved off with Maxey to the spot where they sat every morning before classes began.

"We just sat there talking like a regular day," Maxey later recalled.

A few minutes later, the two teens noticed Luke Woodham enter the Commons area and hand some notebooks to Justin Sledge. They thought nothing of it.

Woodham told Sledge to make sure he passed all

the material to Grant Boyette. Then he advised him to leave the building.

Sledge did not know what the hell he meant at first. But as he watched Woodham's zombielike shuffle back toward the Commons' double doors, he knew something was wrong. Sledge grabbed a friend.

"Go to the library, something very bad is going to happen," said Sledge. "Something very, very, very wrong is going on."

Sledge held on to Woodham's notebooks and headed off toward the library, his friend just ahead of him.

As they moved down the corridor, he told his friend, "Don't look back. Don't look back. No matter what you do, don't look back."

Back out in the parking lot, Luke Woodham was carefully concealing his father's old hunting rifle under his long trench coat before getting out of the Corsica. Finally, he emerged and started walking slowly back toward the double front doors.

Woodham strolled into the Commons, his dad's .30–.30 rifle resting casually on his hip. One eyewitness later said he came through the swinging doors like a cowboy about to have a duel in a saloon.

Josh Maxey saw Woodham walk back through the commons area with what he thought was a nonlethal ROTC training rifle, before suddenly realizing it was real.

"Jesus, that ain't an ROTC rifle," Maxey screamed at Wes Brownell.

The two boys ran for cover behind a huge pillar.

Christy Menefee's best friend, Brook Mitchke, was standing talking to Christy near one of the other pillars in the Commons when she felt a shiver run through her. She looked up.

Luke Woodham was pointing the .30–.30 rifle straight at her. It still rested on his hip. Woodham stared hard at her for a beat, then turned and swung his rifle toward his once-beloved Christy Menefee.

Menefee was talking to another girl and didn't even see the look of despair on his face until it was too late. He caught her in the back with two blasts before she'd gotten two steps away.

The moment Woodham shot Christy, her friend Brook knew immediately why. Christy had been complaining to her for months about Woodham's strange reaction to her ending their relationship.

Brook collapsed on the floor sobbing as she tried to revive her best friend dying on the floor beside her.

David Lawson, fourteen, a ninth grader, was sitting just ten feet away from a group of girl students when Woodham approached. When he first saw the gun, Lawson thought it was a fake. Then he saw what had happened to Christy Menefee.

He and a friend started running. Woodham aimed and fired at Lawson's friend. The bullet ricocheted off the brick post as they scrambled for cover.

Then Woodham aimed at Lawson. He heard the bullet hit his book bag with a thud as it dropped to the floor and literally exploded.

Luke Woodham then turned toward classmate Lydia Dew, who'd also been talking near Christy Menefee. She was scrambling across the slippery black-and-white tile floor. He shot her in the head.

His targeting apparently over, the lone gunman

opened fire randomly on dozens of classmates huddled in terror nearby. He kept firing from the hip, almost as if the finger squeezing on the trigger was not connected to the blank expression on his face.

Sophomore Kimberly Johnson, fifteen, was in the restroom doorway in the Commons when she heard two shots. She turned to see Woodham running across the Commons. She ducked back in the restroom and heard more shots.

Kimberly then rushed to Christina Menefee's side and noticed blood coming from her neck. Her face was blue and pale. Kimberly already knew she must be dead.

When Luke Woodham stopped to reload his rifle, student Jason Barton tried to tackle him. He ran after Woodham, grabbed him, and they grappled for a few seconds until the heavier Woodham pushed Barton off and headed across the hall, his rifle back resting on his hip.

Across the other side of the hall, a coach was directing students out of the building. Tony John, a seventeen-year-old senior, helped one injured student to safety, taking off his own shirt to try to stop the bleeding.

Senior Alan Westbrook heard Woodham shout across at him, "You turned your back on us."

Woodham shot straight at Westbrook's hip. He fell to the ground immediately.

Westbrook later recalled: "I tried to get up, but I couldn't. It was like there were a thousand ants all over my legs."

Tenth-grader Angel Hall, fifteen, was talking in the commons area with several students, including her friend Denise Magee and band teacher Jeff Cannon, when they heard the sound of a gun firing.

"We thought it was the cannon that they shoot at football games," Hall later recalled.

After three more consecutive shots echoed across the hallway, the group turned and began running. Denise Magee was struck by a bullet in the left side of her stomach. She fell to the ground, screaming for her friend Angel.

Pearl High math teacher Heather McKinion was on her way up the stairs to her classroom around eight A.M. when she heard a loud bang and a scream. She immediately turned around and ran back down the steps toward the commons, where she found Christina Menefee lying on the ground, shot through the neck.

Lydia Kay Dew was beside Menefee. Her only visible wound was a bullet wound to her arm. It looked as if the bullet had passed through Menefee's neck and then ricocheted off Dew.

McKinion was convinced Menefee was already dead, but Dew seemed to be all right. Actually, Dew had been shot in the back, but because of the way she was lying, the only wound appeared to be on her arm.

"I never in my life thought I'd have to stand next to someone and watch them die," McKinion later recalled. "Until now."

Pearl High substitute teacher Chip Smith had been standing next to victims Lydia Dew and Christina Menefee in the commons area of the school as youngsters began pouring in for the start of classes.

Seconds earlier, Smith had been discussing schoolwork and going to the state fair with Dew. He didn't even notice Luke Woodham walking toward them.

Smith heard a *boom!* and Dew had dropped to the floor beside him.

He later recalled, "She was alert and still talking about going to the fair. She was trying to talk to someone else, I don't know who. Then she stopped and her eyes rolled back in her head."

Smith is convinced to this day that Woodham knew where Menefee would be and what time she'd be there.

Also standing nearby was seventeen-year-old Deepika Dhawan, a junior at the high school. She was leaning against a wall near the administrative offices when she noticed Woodham walk up to them.

"When he shot, he didn't say anything," she recalled. Deepika did not even realize her two friends had been shot dead.

"All I saw was his face, then black, then a rifle," she later remembered.

She turned and ran for her life, but in the confusion ran straight into a wall. Only then did she feel severe pain in her left shoulder where Woodham's bullet had hit her. Deepika scrambled back on her feet and made it to the bathroom across the hall, where she huddled and cried, too afraid to open the door.

Outside in the commons, Woodham continued firing from the hip.

Stephanie Wiggins, fifteen, a tenth grader, was shot in the left hip and collapsed on the floor.

Jon Palmer, fourteen, a freshman, was shot in the right hip.

Seventeen-year-old sophomore Jerry Safely leaped in front of his girlfriend to try to shield her. He took gunshot wounds to both legs and crashed to the floor.

Safely didn't realize Woodham had mistaken him for another student.

Woodham was so shocked by his mistake, he walked over to Safely and told him he was sorry and that the shot had been meant for Kyle Foster, a junior who'd "dissed" Woodham a few weeks earlier in a school corridor.

Freshman Robert Harris, Jr., fourteen, was hit in the left calf by a spray of bullets. When the shots had started ringing out, all he remembered thinking was "this doesn't happen at Pearl."

When the bullets struck him, it seemed like someone had simply kicked him "very hard."

Harris immediately stumbled toward the school's band hall, and it was only when a friend took a look at his leg that he realized he'd been hit.

Back in the commons area, bullets had struck the floor and fragmented before grazing some students in the legs. A lot of them were superficial wounds and some of the students just kept running across the hallway into another building. They were still running for their lives.

Ninth-grader Tara Yeager, fourteen, was just hanging out as usual in the commons area when "somebody shot a gun," she later recalled.

Tara and her friend Ashley Downs, fifteen, thought it was a firecracker at first. They stopped and looked around. When another shot rang out, the two girls took off running. They later said they heard at least seven more shots before they got out into the parking lot area of the campus.

As they ran out toward the I-20, they dropped their school bags, and one of them even lost one of her sneakers in the panic.

That was when Tara thought, "Why am I running if we're going to be killed anyway? This is it."

Filled with an impending sense of doom, the two teens headed for a small wood beyond the parking lot and kept running. Eventually they saw a car stop and scrambled into it.

Wes Brownell's friend Josh Maxey had absolutely no doubt that Brownell knew nothing about Woodham's plans. He later recalled: "Wes had no idea it was going to happen. Afterwards he was in as much shock as I was."

But Maxey did wonder why Woodham made no attempt to shoot Brownell as he was shooting at virtually everyone else in the commons area.

After what had seemed like dozens of bullets had ripped through lockers and chipped powder kegs of plaster off the walls, as well as cutting down at least nine innocent young people, the shooting stopped. It was exactly eleven minutes since the killer had fired his first shot.

A cloud of dust and cordite wafted through the wall of silence that descended on the scene of carnage. A silence broken only by the sobbing of students kneeling or lying on the vast black-and-white floor.

Gazing through the mist at the bloodshed he had just created, Luke Woodham pointed the barrel down, turned around, and headed back out of the double doors toward the school parking lot.

Fifteen

Pearl High School Assistant Principal Joel Myrick was in his office when he heard the gunshots. He ran out, ushered several students into his office, shutting and locking the door. Then he ran down the corridor toward the commons where he saw the carnage.

"I didn't want to run, but I didn't want to do a headlong rush into him," Myrick later recalled. "There were a million things running through my mind. I knew I couldn't rush him unarmed. But I knew if I didn't do something, he would keep killing."

Myrick went straight to his car in the parking lot and grabbed a .45-caliber pistol he kept in his glove compartment. He loaded it with one bullet and ran to the side of the building where he spotted Woodham leaving with the rifle still in his hand.

Myrick's training as a commander of the 631st Field Artillery Brigade of the Mississippi National Guard based in Grenada was about to come in very useful.

Seconds after Woodham got into the Corsica and fired up the engine, Myrick ran alongside him and ordered him to stop. Woodham looked up, but slammed his foot firmly on the gas pedal.

Myrick pointed his pistol directly at Woodham. His finger on the trigger.

The car's tires squealed as it got some traction and pulled off. Myrick didn't fire.

As Woodham drove away, pandemonium ensued inside the commons. Dozens of students poured out of the huge double doors into the very same parking lot.

Distracted by what was happening, Woodham had only gotten a few yards when his car veered dangerously close to a car driven by Pearl High junior Justin Barnett moving in the opposite direction.

Barnett immediately realized what had happened and slammed his car into reverse and backed up diagonally to block Woodham's car. Woodham pulled the steering wheel to his right, mounted the sidewalk, and headed across a grass verge in the hope he'd get back onto the road once he was past the car that was blocking his route.

But the Corsica sank into the grass and stopped moving. Woodham slammed his foot down on the gas to try to get the car to move, but it was completely stuck. The Corsica's tires spun furiously as Woodham sat like a sitting duck in the driver's seat.

Assistant Principal Myrick once again got alongside the car and this time pointed his .45 right inside the open driver's window, pressing it into Woodham's neck. This time he was prepared to press the trigger. Woodham was shaking from side to side. For a moment, the teen kept his foot on the gas pedal and the tires kept spinning. The only reason Myrick didn't squeeze the trigger was because he knew the car was going nowhere.

Woodham then sat there staring into space, tears welling up in his eyes as the enormity of what he had just done began to dawn on him.

"Get out the car and lie on the ground—*now!*" screamed Myrick.

The tires stopped spinning and Woodham put his hands above his head. He didn't want to die.

As Woodham got out, Myrick pulled Woodham's coat over his head, pushed him to the ground, and jammed his foot on the teenager's back to stop him from moving.

"Why?" said Myrick, "Why? Why?"

Woodham didn't respond right away. Then he said, "Mr. Myrick, I was the guy who gave you the discount on the pizza the other night."

Myrick was stunned. What the hell was he talking about?

Woodham told Myrick the world had treated him badly.

"Well, wait 'til you get to Parchman," said Myrick, referring to the state correctional institution.

Myrick would have shot Woodham without hesitation if the teen had tried to escape.

"I think he's a coward, and I had my weapon pointed at his head and he didn't want to die," Myrick recalled.

Myrick was convinced Woodham might have committed more killings if he had managed to flee the campus. Myrick even feared for the safety of his son, a student at Pearl Junior High, just a couple of miles away.

"I just thought he's killing people," Myrick later told reporters. "But I forgive him [Woodham] because he's a human being. I don't hold grudges."

A long road leads from the main U.S. 80 into Pearl High School. When parent Keith Warren approached the ninety-degree curve in the road just before the bus-loading area, he saw people running away from the parking lot.

Warren's first thought was that some kind of fight had erupted on the school campus. Then he remembered back to his own days in high school when everyone flocked to a fight, not away from one. That's when he got really concerned.

Around the next curve in the long winding road, his fear turned to reality. Warren and his daughter Ashley noticed masses of students pouring out of the school. Luke Woodham was walking from the school building after the shooting, and they watched as he rounded the back of a white Corsica and began to open the driver's door.

"That guy's got a gun!" Ashley, sitting next to him, screamed.

Warren only then noticed Woodham was carrying what looked like a shotgun or maybe a rifle. The strange thing was the teen didn't seem in a hurry or panicked. Warren watched as Woodham opened the car door and placed the gun inside.

Suddenly it dawned on Warren that he and his daughter were in range of the shooter. The next few minutes were, in his words, "surreal."

Warren's first thought at that minute was to get away from the lone gunman as fast as he could. He punched the accelerator and turned into the parking lot where dozens of people were gathering.

It was only after he'd gotten far enough away to be out of range of the gunman that Warren switched hats from concerned parent to journalist. He parked his car and started asking questions.

Warren spotted two teens in a car who'd been shot

and were being attended by adults. One boy was sitting in the driver's seat, nursing a wound to his calf. A girl in the backseat of the vehicle was crying. Warren couldn't clearly see what injuries she had sustained, but she was obviously in pain.

"D'you know who he was?" asked Warren.

"His name's Lucas. He was in my class about four years ago," answered the injured teen, who was trying to stop the bleeding from his leg. The boy said he couldn't remember the shooter's last name.

Warren knew he was in the middle of a big story and needed to tell his paper, the *Clarion-Ledger* in nearby Jackson, what was happening, but he also wanted to get his daughter off the campus and into a safe environment.

He got back in his car and drove slowly back onto the street, constantly on the lookout for the gunman. To the left, he noticed the white car from earlier had skidded off the road and come to a halt on a grassy verge.

Police began pouring onto the campus and students were running, sirens wailing, and school buses had screeched to a halt all along the road to the school entrance. The kids who were running had fear, excitement, tears, and shock etched all over their faces.

A man stepped in front of Warren's car and ordered him to stop the vehicle until the ambulances had come through.

Inside the car Warren's daughter Ashley was crying for her closest friends Ashley and Tara. All three were cheerleaders and spent virtually all their free time together. Warren looked in his rear-view mirror and noticed Ashley and Tara running down the road toward her car. Warren shouted at them to get in immediately.

Ashley was as white as a sheet; Tara was crying.

Warren took his daughter, her two friends, and a boy they'd never met before to Ashley's parents' house, before he headed out to his newspaper office.

Sixteen

More than 70 law-enforcement officers converged on the Pearl High campus and its 1600 students within minutes of the shooting. As well as local police, there were state troopers and officers from nearby Brandon, Palahatchie, Flowood, and the Rankin County Sheriff's Department. They were swiftly followed by a fleet of ambulances and a host of paramedics.

One of the first police officers on the scene was Captain George Burgess of the Pearl Police Department (PPD). The dispatcher had said something about shots being fired and people being down.

After twenty-four years in the PPD, Burgess suspected it might have been a crank call, as the only sort of problems that had occurred at Pearl High involved a little dope smoking at worst.

Nothing could have prepared him for the scene that greeted him as his white police cruiser slued into the parking lot.

Assistant Principal Joel Myrick was standing over a teen sprawled out on the grassy verge alongside a white compact with its driver's door hanging open. And Myrick was pointed a pistol down at the teen on the ground.

Burgess quickly ascertained that the teen was the shooter.

Pearl Police Detective Roy Dampier arrived on the scene. At twenty-five, Dampier was considered an officer with a rosy future. Earlier that year, while still in uniform, he'd set an impressive PPD record with 115 arrests for driving while under the influence over the previous twelve months. DUIs had been front-page news in Pearl. They wouldn't be anymore.

Dampier headed straight for Myrick and Woodham. The teen remained glued to the ground, too scared to move a muscle in case he was shot. Dampier leaned down, pulled Woodham's wrists together, and cuffed him.

Then he hauled the teen to his feet, placed him under arrest, frisked him, and found more ammo. Dampier bundled Woodham into the back of a PPD cruiser, where he was read his rights immediately.

Detective Dampier was surprised how calm Luke Woodham seemed. Dampier also later noted that his prisoner never once mentioned demons or Grant Boyette.

"He said his girlfriend was the reason behind all this and he shot everyone else because they were just there," Dampier said.

Neither Dampier nor any of the other police officers at the scene noticed the cut on Woodham's hand immediately after he was arrested.

With the shooter under lock and key, police scrambled to secure the crime scene, calm fleeing students, and control traffic backups created by parents racing to the campus to see if their children were safe.

Back inside the school, a terrified Deepika Dhawan finally plucked up the courage to step slowly out of the bathroom. Emergency personnel were arriving in the commons area and she realized her arm was soaked with blood.

The most seriously injured students were taken by ambulance to the Rankin Medical Center, just five miles away on U.S. 80 in Brandon. Two of the less-injured victims were diverted to the next closest emergency room at River Oaks Hospital on Lakeland Drive in Flowood, seven miles from the school. Two other injured students were ferried in private vehicles to the Rankin Medical Center.

A few hundred yards up the street from the campus, Kyle Foster was stuck in traffic, completely unaware that he had been one of Luke Woodham's intended targets. Woodham had wanted revenge for the shoving match between the two teens a couple of months earlier.

Mississippi Governor Kirk Fordice immediately appealed to area law-enforcement agencies, urging them to lend manpower to the city of Pearl. Fordice was careful to emphasize that he issued the appeal because of the magnitude of the crime—not because he thought the Pearl Police couldn't handle the situation.

In nearby Brandon, Police Chief Eugene Adcock sent all but two of his officers to Pearl High.

"They didn't know what they were getting into, so we wanted to help in any way we could," Adcock explained. "We're just sorry we couldn't do more."

Minutes after the arrest of Luke Woodham, dozens of Pearl High students gathered at the intersection of U.S. 80 and Pirate Cove to console and comfort each other. They were anxious for answers, but were barred by officers from the Mississippi Highway Patrol, Pearl

Police Department, and Rankin County Sheriff's Department from entering the school grounds.

They started telling each other about the horrors they'd just witnessed on campus.

"I saw him with the gun in his hands and thought to myself, 'Oh, shit,'" said Nathan Henry, a ninth grader. "I sat there and saw him shoot three or four times and then I ran out the door. When I went back up, I saw people lying everywhere."

His voice breaking into sobs, he said he didn't know if any of the victims were his friends. "I am trying to get back up there."

He remembered one particular classmate. "I don't know if he got out. Everybody I saw looked dead."

Many parents were standing on the grass verge entrance to the school road determined not to let their children out of their sight.

Inside the school commons area, police were greeted by scenes that looked like something out of a war movie: Students lay sprawled out on the black-and-white tile floor, and at first glance, it looked as if the gunman had mowed down dozens. Books and book bags, even shoes, lay sprawled across the floor. Bullets had ricocheted off the pillars leaving a residue of dust. On other parts of the floor were spatterings of blood.

Out in the parking lot area, Mary Anne Woodham's Corsica stood slued across the grass verge. Inside, the .30–.30 Marlin lever-action rifle lay on the front passenger seat. The front driver's door remained open where Assistant Principal Joel Myrick had ordered the teen gunman out of the car.

Back inside the commons area, paramedics were treating the injured. It was already too late to help Christy Menefee and her friend Lydia Dew. Menefee had taken fatal shots just below her throat at the clavicle and in the left shoulder, while Dew had extensive wounds to the head, the underside of the upper arm, and the torso.

Investigators had already recovered an envelope containing thirty more live rounds of .30–.30 ammo in Luke Woodham's pocket before he was taken away.

Rankin County Sheriff's Investigator Greg Eklund was also one of the first on the scene after getting a call at home at just past eight A.M. His job was to make an initial preliminary examination of the crime scene. After twenty-five years in law enforcement and a member of the Rankin County criminal investigations department since 1993, there wasn't much Greg Eklund hadn't seen in his long and distinguished career. He was proud of having attended a crime-scene school at Sirchie Crime Scene Technologies, in Raleigh, North Carolina.

Just a few weeks before the Pearl High shootings, he'd attended a crime-scene training school in Biloxi, Mississippi, which had been held in conjunction with the Institution of Police Technology Management. Eklund had been taught over a number of years to observe crime scenes in a way most other police officers couldn't.

But on the morning of October 1, 1997, Greg Eklund was exhausted from an all-night stakeout. He'd only made it home just an hour before the call from a dispatcher.

Eklund had no idea that the shooting was inside the school. He'd assumed it had taken place in the parking lot. The investigator had teenage children and even came originally from Pearl, but had moved several years before the shooting to the rural community of Florence, Mississippi. However, he knew many kids at Pearl because some of them played soccer with his son.

"I knew, based on the radio traffic, that we did have kids down, but I didn't realize until I got to the school that it was actually inside the building," he said.

Greg Eklund did not return home for the following thirty-six hours.

Eklund went through the double doors of the commons tentatively, having been warned by other officers to expect the worst.

"The first word you can think of would be 'chaos.' That was followed by a sense of terror because there were clothing items left abandoned by kids. Some of them had literally run out of their shoes with fear."

Eklund saw book bags and jewelry scattered all over the place. There was "a great deal of blood and, of course, the two victims," he said.

By this time the entire building had been vacated. An eerie silence fell over the scene. In some ways that made it seem more surreal to Eklund.

"These kids had run to classrooms and shut the door. They'd run outside through the parking lots. They'd just run for their lives," he explained.

The only fit and healthy living person from within the school that Eklund encountered was Assistant Principal Joel Myrick. There were also a handful of police officers containing the crime scene.

Eklund walked over to where the two teenage girls had been so coldly blasted to their deaths. He crouched down and looked at them.

"To see these two dead young girls was awful," he later said. "I had to step back and catch my breath. I knew I had to do my job, but it wasn't easy."

Over the following half-hour, Eklund and his colleagues began preserving all the evidence they could find, including the casings from the .30–.30 rifle and the bullets that were scattered across the tile floor. In all, Detective Eklund covered the scene four times just to be sure he'd collected everything.

Back outside in a PPD cruiser, arresting officer Roy Dampier spotted Woodham taking tape off his hands, which were both covered around the palms. As Woodham removed the tape, Dampier noticed a large cut on one of his hands.

"How'd you cut your hands, Luke?" asked Dampier.

Woodham paused for a moment, then looked up at the detective and spoke in a low voice.

"Killing my mom . . ."

"Killing your mom?" replied Dampier.

Woodham then told the officer he had attacked her with a knife earlier that morning at their home and that she was "probably dead."

Until that moment, no one had given a thought to the possibility that Luke Woodham might have harmed another person besides the students at Pearl High. Dampier remained puzzled by Woodham's calm appearance. He seemed so cool and almost proud of what he'd done, the officer later recalled.

As soon as there was a break in radio traffic, Dampier contacted his control room and told them to get over to the Woodham home as quickly as possible. Moments later, Roy Dampier's colleague Detective Aaron Hirschfield arrived on the scene and took over responsibility for the prisoner who was about to be driven to the Pearl Police Department for questioning.

Seventeen

At 8:20 A.M., three officers, including Pearl Police Department Sergeant John McCoy, entered the home on Barrow Street and went straight to the main bedroom where they found Mary Anne Woodham's body. McCoy covered the body and told the other officers not to touch anything until the crime-lab boys got to the scene.

When Detective Don Manning arrived, Sergeant McCoy told him the body was in the back bedroom. As Manning walked past Luke Woodham's bedroom, he noticed several items lying on top of the bed, so he went in and examined them. One was the old hickory knife the teen had used in his attack on his mother. Another was an aluminum baseball bat caked in blood.

Manning walked into the main bedroom and carefully pulled back the sheet to look down at the battered and punctured corpse lying on top of the bed.

Less than a mile away from the high school, victim Lydia Dew's mom, Kaye Long, heard about the shooting from some neighbors as she walked into her house. It was about 8:30 A.M. She grabbed her handbag and leaped in her car to rush to the school to pick up her daughter.

Kaye was met by school officials who led her through the yellow crime-scene tape that by now surrounded the entrance to the school by the big rear parking lot.

Walking in through the double doors, Long saw a body covered by a white sheet. "I knew it was her. I didn't want to believe it, but I just knew," she remembered.

Kaye Long stopped in the bloody hallway and tried to contain herself. The words of the school officials and police investigators were not fully registering.

She heard the name "Luke Woodham" mentioned. She knew him well. He had attended the prom with Lydia's older sister, Lea Ann, when she was a junior and he was a freshman at Pearl High two years previously.

Kaye Long collapsed in floods of tears.

With Luke Woodham in the backseat of the police cruiser, two officers drove through a crowd of reporters pushing and jostling for a picture. Woodham kept his head down and remained silent. Neither of the police officers said a word. They did not want to say anything that might be later construed to be improper or coercive.

At the Pearl police station, just a five-minute walk from the Woodham home on Brewer Street, Luke Woodham was taken into the day room, not a cell. It was a large area with gray metal tables fixed to the floor, with seats like picnic tables.

"It is a completely secure room, but we wanted to

protect him from contact with anybody," explained one officer.

Luke was immediately told he would be charged on three counts of murder and seven of aggravated assault.

Within minutes of arrival in the building, Luke Woodham waived his rights and began writing—in his own childish scrawl—a statement about the events at Pearl High.

It read:

> At 7:50 A.M., I got into the car, went up to the school, and gave my messages to Justin Sledge. I went back to the car, got the gun, and went to the school. I ran up to Christine Menefee and shot her. I turned and shot Lydia Dew. I fired into the air and must have shot Stephanie Wiggins.
>
> I turned to Alan Westbrook and shot him three times. I told Jerry Safely that I wouldn't hurt him because he had never harmed. I ran down the hall and ran on to the front door. I jumped back into the car, sped off, and ran off the road. Mr. Myrick pulled his gun on me and I gave up.

Toward the end of the statement, Woodham's writing became increasingly erratic and his signature at the bottom of the page was virtually illegible.

Woodham was led away to have a mugshot taken. Still wearing his wide-rimmed glasses, Luke Woodham looked remarkably unworried as he stood in front of the camera.

After that, Woodham agreed to a videotaped interview that would later provide many with the ultimate insight into his behavior on that tragic morning. He once again waived his right to a lawyer.

The statement was witnessed by Rankin County Detective Aaron Hirschfield, who made sure Woodham signed a video release form.

As the officer later explained: "I want them [people under arrest] to understand that the interview is going to be videotaped and I want them to understand it can be used for training purposes and that it will be used in a court of law if necessary."

Woodham's taped statement began: "I woke up this morning. I got a butcher knife and a pillow. I got into my mother's room at about five A.M. I put the pillow over her head and stabbed her."

At one point, Woodham looked up at Detective Hirschfield and declared, "I'm not insane, sir. I knew what I was doing. I was just pissed at the time."

One psychiatric expert later testified that Woodham's behavior throughout the taped interview was not bizarre or peculiar in any way. He claimed that Woodham's personality at the time and during later stringent tests did not even suggest he was suffering from a psychotic disorder.

Woodham's claim that he'd been having hallucinations for at least six to eight months before the shootings and that they stopped at the moment of his arrest did not ring true either.

Perhaps just as significantly, Woodham made a comment to investigators toward the end of the interview that seemed to put a completely different slant on the case. Woodham implied he'd killed his mother because it was the only way he could get to borrow her car.

* * *

At nine-thirty A.M., Rankin County Sheriff's Department Special Investigator Greg Eklund arrived at the Woodham family home to start what he knew would be a painstaking and at times harrowing examination of the last morning of Mary Anne Woodham's life.

The Rankin County Sheriff's Department is rightly proud of its Mobile Crime Lab—a unit specifically designed for working violent crime scenes. The lab is equipped with scientific and chemical equipment that can be used to enhance and gather all types of forensic evidence, however minute.

On board the mobile lab there was even an alternative light source to provide lighting that could help detect different types of minute fibers at crime scenes simply by making the area dark. Eklund also had available to him various chemical agents that could detect a whole range of body fluids.

The mobile unit was positioned around the front porch to the house and the entire area was quickly roped off with yellow crime-scene tape, extending from the front right down one side of the property.

Eklund donned sterile latex gloves before unlocking the front door with a key provided to investigators by Luke Woodham. The area they stepped into contained a washing machine and dryer to the left of the doorway. Eklund moved into the kitchen, noting the refrigerator, stove, and sink, then walked into the dining area, which held a table with some chairs around it. So far, it seemed like thousands of other homes throughout the community.

But Greg Eklund wasn't interested in domesticity. He was examining every surface looking for blood evidence. His walk through the house wasn't much different from the one a real-estate broker might take, but with one big difference—he was constantly on the lookout for evidence of murder.

The first drop of blood Eklund found was in the area by the entrance to the kitchen and the utility room alongside it. Eklund photographed the evidence and moved on. It was the first of eighteen such pictures he took that disturbing morning.

As the investigator entered the kitchen and dining room area, there was a small bar that extended out from the wall with a phone on it. A bloody bandage rested there. He immediately bagged it.

Eklund next saw bloodstains on the doorjamb. He photographed them. Then he sprayed some of the chemical Luminar on areas that seemed to have bloodstains. The chemical reacts to the presence of blood, causing it to luminesce eerily. Next he cut up a section of the dining room carpet that had specks of blood on it and bagged it.

He located the silver aluminum baseball bat Luke Woodham had used to beat his mother into submission.

Then it was time to enter the biggest scene of bloody carnage—Mary Anne Woodham's bedroom. His job was not to examine the body—that was for the coroner. Eklund worked his way around Mary Anne's corpse, looking for evidence.

Eklund found what he later called "quite a bit of bloodletting" on the bed. More than six feet up on one of the walls there were also tiny specks of blood. Behind the bed he found another sizable blood splatter. Eklund continued photographing every wall and item as he went along.

At 9:45 A.M., Mary Anne Woodham's bruised and

punctured body was removed from the family home by Rankin County Medical Examiner's technicians.

Greg Eklund and his colleagues continued their search for clues as to how Mary Anne Woodham was killed.

Eklund's step-by-step examination of the Barrow Street house soon told him what had happened earlier that morning. He'd already been briefed about Woodham's initial statement claiming that his mom had been asleep at the moment he killed her. Everything Eklund saw told him the opposite.

"What I saw told me that Mrs. Woodham was up that morning and she almost made it to the kitchen and at that point some kind of violent attack commenced at that area and I believe Luke went into that bedroom and stabbed her."

Eklund concluded that Woodham's initial assault on his mother had begun in the hallway next to the kitchen.

"I really believe in my heart that Mrs. Woodham ran back to her bedroom to try and get away from what was happening and he followed her into the bedroom and she was killed in the bed," Eklund said.

Eklund's examination also told him something about family life inside that house.

"You didn't see many of the family photos you would normally see," he later recalled. "It was an unloved house in many ways."

In fact the only thing that took any pride of place was the framed photo of Mary Anne with her two sons that Luke so avidly detested.

Eklund found Luke Woodham's bedroom to be typical of a teenage boy's. He wanted to find out more about Woodham's specific musical tastes, but there

160 **Jon Bellini**

were few clues. As Eklund later explained, "I wanted to look, verify, isolate, and quarantine various items."

In those early stages of the investigation, it seemed that a lonely teen fed up with his life had turned into a homicidal maniac. That conviction helped some in the community come to terms with the tragedy, for it created a measure of sympathy for the sad, lonely existence of the gunman.

Outside the Woodham house there was a feeling of genuine loss on Brewer Street. Though the property was cordoned off by yellow crime-scene ribbon, floral tributes and notes had been laid down by neighbors. Rivulets of brightly colored wax littered the driveway where candles had been placed as a memorial to the tragedy. A wreath trimmed in pink ribbon stood in the front yard of the house. IN REMEMBRANCE OF MARY ANNE WOODHAM, it read.

Victim Christina Menefee, 16, was the first student
Luke Woodham, 16, shot.

Lydia Dew, 16, was an unplanned victim of
Woodham's shooting spree.

Pearl High School in Pearl, Mississippi was the site of
Woodham's October 1, 1997 shooting rampage.

Police collect evidence in the Commons, Pearl High's
front hall, where most of the students were shot.
(*Photo courtesy Rankin County, MS Sheriff's Department*)

Bullet hole in pillar of the Commons. (*Photo courtesy Rankin County, MS Sheriff's Department*)

Assistant Principal Joel Myrick detained the armed Woodham after the shooting until police arrived. (*Photo courtesy Jackson, MS* Clarion-Ledger)

Home where Luke
Woodham lived with
his mother and
older brother.

Mary Anne Woodham
and her son Luke in
1991. (*Photo courtesy
Rankin County, MS
Sheriff's Department*)

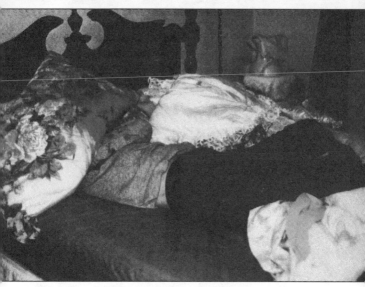

Police found the body of Mary Anne Woodham, 50, in her bedroom after the shooting at Pearl High School. (*Photo courtesy Rankin County, MS Sheriff's Department*)

Aluminum baseball bat Woodham used to bludgeon his mother before stabbing her to death.

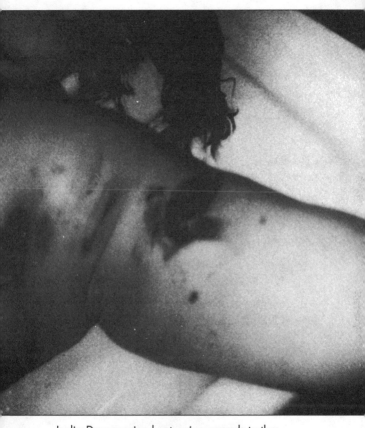

Lydia Dew received extensive wounds to the
underside of the upper arm and torso.
(*Photo courtesy Rankin County, MS Sheriff's Department*)

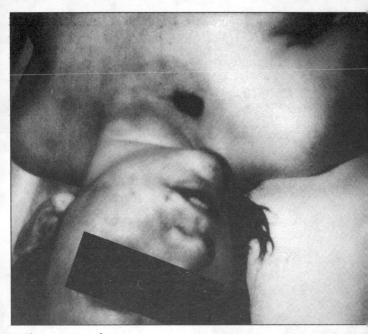

Christina Menefee was fatally shot just below her throat. (*Photo courtesy Rankin County, MS Sheriff's Department*)

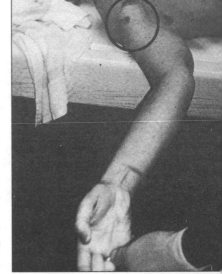

Menefee was also shot in the left shoulder. (*Photo courtesy Rankin County, MS Sheriff's Department*)

Woodham used a .30-.30 Marlin hunting rifle to shoot students at Pearl High.

Luke Woodham a few months before the 1997 shooting.

Woodham was charged with three counts of murder and seven counts of aggravated assault.
(*Photo courtesy Rankin County, MS Sheriff's Department*)

Marshall Grant Boyette, 18, leader of the Kroth
(a role-playing game group Woodham belonged to),
eventually pleaded guilty to conspiracy.
Photo courtesy Rankin County, MS Sheriff's Department

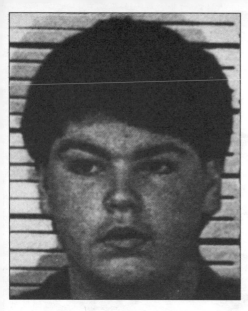

Daniel Lucas Thompson, 16, was one of the Kroth. He testified with immunity in closed court. (*Photo courtesy Forrest County Court, MS*)

Charges against regular Kroth member Delbert Alan Shaw, 18, were dropped after Woodham was convicted. (*Photo courtesy Forrest County Court, MS*)

Originally arrested in conjunction with the shooting, Kroth member Justin Sledge, 16, was later exonerated by Woodham. (*Photo courtesy* Clarion-Ledger)

Woodham being escorted to Rankin County jail in bullet-resistant vest. (*Photo courtesy* Clarion-Ledger)

Notice posted outside Pearl High the day after shooting. (*Photo courtesy Rankin County, MS Sheriff's Department*)

Christina

They took Alan, Wes, Justin, Donnie, Lucas, Grant, and Luke.

This is what happens.

We told you not to leave Al. Or there'd be some shit.

They've removed 1/4 of our army, but they'll pay soon enough.

THE END IS NEAR...APOCALYPSE NOW.

Sincerly,

The Alliance of the

⚡

Immortalz

think what you want-Lydia was no accident.

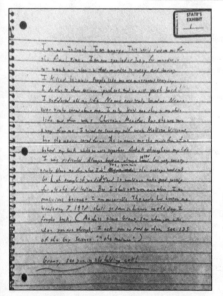

Page from Woodham's five-page "manifesto" written prior to the shooting. (*Photo courtesy Rankin County, MS Sheriff's Department*)

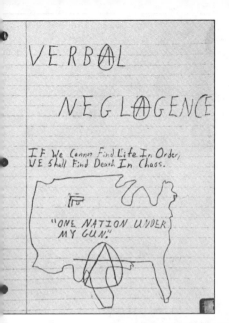

Two of the notes found by investigators in Woodham's bedroom. *(Photo courtesy Rankin County, MS Sheriff's Department)*

Pearl Police Chief
Bill Slade.

Local journalist and
parent of Pearl High
School student, Andy
Kanengisar was one of
the first people on the
scene after the shooting.

Eighteen

At the Rankin Medical Center, victims' classmates and relatives visited the emergency room in waves. Many wept in corners, while others greeted each other with hugs of sympathy. Some formed lines at pay phones to keep their loved ones informed of students' conditions.

Stephanie Wiggins, a tenth grader who had suffered a gunshot wound to the left hip, underwent almost immediate surgery to clean the wound.

Over at the high school, parents were anxious that the shootings might make their children too scared to go to school.

Bobby Williamson, pastor of the Park Place Baptist Church, in Pearl, got a call from the school requesting as many ministers who could get down to the campus as soon as possible. Williamson never forgot the feeling of psychic sickness when he saw the pain and hurt on the faces of the students, and especially the teachers.

"There is no way we can explain or understand this. I hurt for the kids. Their lives will never be the same," he said.

On television sets across the nation, millions were waking up to the awful events in Pearl. A feeling of shock and disbelief swept the country. How could such a terrible thing happen in the most civilized country on earth?

One of those viewers was thirty-eight-year-old Sheila Jeffers. She had never even heard of Pearl, Mississippi, until that awful morning. It was the day her daughter Christy Menefee died in a hail of bullets.

"I kept thinking, 'No, it's not her. It's not her—they are mistaken.' I still think it's a bad dream, I'll wake up and Christy will be fine."

Jeffers, from Prairieville, Louisiana, just outside Baton Rouge, hadn't seen or heard from her daughter Christy Menefee for four years. It seemed that Luke Woodham wasn't the only one with an unfortunate family history. Sheila Jeffers had thought her daughter was still living in Jacksonville, Florida, where the Menefees had resided before moving to Pearl. The family snapshots flashing across the television screen that morning of October 1 were the only pictures she had seen of her daughter since their estrangement.

As Sheila Jeffers watched the story unfold, she saw her ex-husband and his new wife, Annette, grieving, while her loss went unnoticed. Jeffers was angry at seeing Annette portrayed as her daughter's mother.

"I felt betrayed. I not only lost my daughter physically, but they were trying to take all my memories, too. Trying to take my parental rights."

Two hours into the investigation, police still assumed the killings were the work of a lonely, obese teenager with a grudge against the world.

The community of Pearl even showed a level of sympathy for the killer, despite the horrendous nature of his crimes. He'd led an isolated, difficult life brought up by a domineering, overbearing single mother.

"We felt for Luke because he must have been so unhappy to commit such an awful crime," said one Pearl parent to a local television reporter just a couple of hours after the shootings.

It seemed that Luke Woodham was a victim like all the others . . . in a sense. But by lunchtime, investigators talking to Pearl High students and teachers began hearing rumors about a group of teens who knew all about Luke Woodham's deadly plans.

That afternoon, Woodham's onetime friend Wes Brownell went to the Pearl Police Department and told detectives about his friendship with Luke Woodham and the role-playing games masterminded by Grant Boyette.

"Wes pretty much said right there that he did know these people, but he got out of it back in May because I think he didn't want what has happened," Brownell's best friend, Josh Maxey, later explained.

Then another group member, Justin Sledge, went to police and showed them the "troubling" letter Woodham had handed him after arriving at the school and just minutes before the fatal shootings.

Pearl Police Chief Bill Slade described the note as a "manifesto" at the first Pearl High School tragedy news conference, held just a few hours after the killings. Slade revealed to reporters that Woodham's "manifesto" also referred to the breakup of his friendship with Christy Menefee. He said that Woodham described himself as feeling angry and considered that she had treated him unfairly.

Based on that note and the manner in which Woodham killed his mother and then shot dead and injured his schoolmates, Chief Slade reached a chilling conclusion.

"This is not a spontaneous incident," he said. "Woodham had this planned."

Meanwhile, Pearl Schools Superintendent Bill Dodds, under siege by the world's press to reveal details about Woodham, could only say, "We can't find any problems at this time. He is not a known disciplinary problem."

Dr. Steven Hayne, designated pathologist at the state medical examiner's office, came up with some startling findings as he examined the remains of Mary Anne Woodham at the nearby Jackson Coroner's Lab.

Some of the slash wounds to her hands and arms clearly indicated that she had desperately tried to defend herself from her son's murderous attack. On Mary Anne Woodham's left hand were three slash wounds, and on the right hand five more. Luke Woodham's mother had certainly fought a brave battle.

A slash wound is produced by a cutting weapon only on the surface of the skin. If the depth of the wound is no deeper than the injury on the skin surface, then it is classified as a slash wound.

The nature of these wounds clearly indicated that the knife was dragged across the skin surface, as opposed to being driven into the tissue itself. In other words, the killer had been somewhat reluctant.

Three actual stab wounds to the chest were what finally killed Mary Anne Woodham, but she had also been beaten with a blunt object, leaving contusions to her face and body.

The wounds inflicted by Woodham indicated "an

awful lot of anger." The number and frequency of those wounds indicated what a highly emotional state the teen was in at the time of the attack.

After his initial examination, Dr. Hayne used a rape kit as was standard procedure in any crime in which a woman was brutally killed. The results returned from the Mississippi State Crime Lab showed that no sexual assault had taken place.

At the home of victim Lydia Dew, it was dawning on her family that they knew shooter Luke Woodham well. Lydia's stepfather, Mike Long, recalled, "I'd met him a few times when he came to the house. He was a nice guy."

Long felt the natural urge to tell the world what a wonderful child Lydia had been. "We're doing things the way we felt Lydia would want it," he said. "She wouldn't want a bunch of sensationalism or a lot of names and anger being thrown at anyone else. You know, she'd probably be the first one to hug Luke's neck and say, 'I know you didn't mean to do it.' That was the kind of person she was. She saw the good in everybody."

The Longs spent much of the day receiving well-wishers. Tears rose in everyone's eyes whenever Lydia Dew was referred to in the present tense.

Her sister Lea Ann found it especially hard because she was the one who'd shown pity for lonely, shy Luke Woodham and given him rides to school and even escorted him to the prom.

Lea Ann found it very difficult to even enter her sister's room because there were so many reminders; figurines and posters of Lydia's favorite animal—a unicorn—shared space with a children's Bible, a *Space Jam* movie poster, and two racks of clothing. A cockatiel called Yo-Yo sat on a perch inside its cage.

"She was trying to teach him to talk. He never got further than . . ." Lea Ann Dew let out a piercing wolf whistle. She couldn't speak anymore.

Lydia had also been a competitive weightlifter, who could bench press 110 pounds. She was known as "Taz" by her friends and family.

Stepfather Mike Long added, "Lydia didn't cull anyone as a friend—black, white, blue, green, rich, or poor. If you needed something, she would help. She was in the wrong place at the wrong time, but there's no comfort in that for us."

Not surprisingly, Pearl High suspended classes until the following Monday and set aside the rest of the week to help students and teachers deal with the appalling tragedy. Many of the victims and their parents who needed to be counseled in the immediate hours following the atrocity were seen at Pearl Police Department.

Most Pearl High students felt disbelief, anger, and shock about the shootings. As Angela Gaddis, clinical social worker at Life Change Counseling Center in nearby Jackson, explained, "It's okay to talk about it, and its okay if they need counseling. They don't have to be ashamed or feel like they have to pretend everything is okay."

Pearl High English teacher Peggy Burke, whose two daughters went to the school, attended a special mass just hours after the rampage, to help deal with the grief.

"It will take God's help to get through this," she said. "I knew Lydia. She was a very nice girl, a very loving person."

The community was trying to rally together. But they were about to be severely put to the test. High school Assistant Principal Joel Myrick—already hailed a hero for disarming the gunman—had an insightful take on why the shooting might have happened.

He said, "Kids are hanging on monkey bars with weak arms and nobody is there to catch them when they fall. We have to work on the reasons kids pick up guns to kill."

Nineteen

Rumors linking Woodham to a group involved in alleged Satanic activities, combined with the statements of the two Pearl teens, convinced Rankin County District Attorney John Kitchens that he was onto something.

He urged the Pearl Police Department and the county sheriff's department to step up their investigation following the Pearl High outrage.

John Kitchens—a man who'd always considered himself a soldier fighting in the trenches of the war on crime—could smell blood. The aftermath of the Pearl shootings made him completely change his battle plan because it was clearly not like any other crime he had ever come across.

The forty-seven-year-old married father of three and resident of nearby Ridgeland was considered a passionate courtroom scrapper and a tenacious investigator for the truth.

A brief outline of his background might explain why. For five years Kitchens had worked as a high school teacher, and then as a police officer in neighboring Lee County after graduating from Mississippi State University. Kitchens later earned his law degree from the University of Mississippi School of Law.

"I find John to be very aggressive in the courtroom,

but any attorney who is in court is adversarial, but I've never had a problem getting along with him," explained local lawyer John Chapman.

John Kitchens prided himself on being a "tough on crime" advocate and at one time had a policy of no plea bargains for house burglars. But in the hours after the Pearl High shootings even he sounded emotional when he told the media, "It's a tragic situation for this community. It'll take a long time for the community of Pearl to get over this. We're all in shock. Pearl is a good place to live and raise a family."

John Kitchens saw it as his duty to make sure there was a rapid return to that feeling of security and happiness that had enveloped Pearl for so many years until Luke Woodham decided to take revenge on society.

On Wednesday evening, the heartbroken families of victims Christy Menefee and Lydia Dew gathered at the Baldwin-Lee Funeral Home, in Pearl. Reporters who tried to interview them were told to go away.

Less than a mile away, many Pearl High students shared testimonies at the Eastside Baptist Church, in Pearl. Over at the Park Place Baptist Church, about seventy more high school teenagers entered the sanctuary of the church and testified. Almost two hundred adults were also in attendance to encourage and pray with them. Some were parents, others teachers and area residents. Other churches in the city were just as busy.

"We hope to begin the healing process now," said the Reverend Ted Dukes, pastor of the Paul Truitt Memorial Baptist Church. "We lift up the families that

CHILD'S PREY   171

have been devastated by what has happened at the school."

Those attending the service at the Paul Truitt Memorial Baptist Church joined hands and asked God to strengthen the families of the deceased, heal those who were injured, and protect the students throughout the school year.

Pearl resident Mary Brookins summed up the attitude of many in the community when she said: "Sometimes we get angry with God when things like this happen, but we shouldn't. Things like this happen for a reason. We just have to accept what God allows and move on from there."

That Wednesday evening, local lawyer Richard H. Wilson went with his family to the local state fairground in a numbed condition like most of the community. When he got home, he got a call from the Rankin County Clerk.

"We'd like you to represent Luke at his initial appearance in the morning."

Wilson responded, "And to what do I owe that honor? I thought y'all liked me?"

"The judge is real nervous and wanted somebody who is familiar with how these things work," she replied.

Meanwhile, even more detailed stories were circulating in Pearl about a group of high school outcasts who'd devised a "hit list" of kids from prominent families whom Woodham and others had targeted.

Investigators, led by county DA John Kitchens, were now convinced that others were involved, but they didn't want to make any moves until they were absolutely certain.

Sometime in the middle of that Wednesday night, a chilling note was pinned up outside the entrance to the school.

It read:

CHRISTINA
They took Alan, Wes, Justin, Donnie
Lucas, Grant, and Luke.
This is what happens.
We told you not to leave A1 Or
there'd be some shit.
They've removed 1/4 of our army, but
they'll pay soon enough.
THE END IS NEAR . . . APOCALYPSE NOW.
Sincerely,
The Alliance of the
Immortalz

think what you want—Lydia was no accident.

The note stunned and upset high school staff who arrived at the campus early Thursday morning. It was immediately handed over to investigators to be analyzed for prints and any other clues as to who had written it.

Detectives considered the note to be more than just some teen prank in poor taste. To DA John Kitchens, it looked like yet more evidence of some sort of conspiracy behind the crimes committed by Luke Woodham.

"That note geared us up. We had documentation indicating there were more out there," said county investigator Greg Eklund.

That same morning, Thursday, October 2, Luke Woodham's newly appointed legal counsel Richard H. Wilson went to the Pearl PD offices and made copies of the three counts of murder and seven of aggravated assault. Then Wilson made a quick outline of how the case had progressed to give to Woodham before having his first meeting with his client.

Wilson's take on the youngster was fascinating. "He was very agitated, angry, pumped up, still very aggressive," Wilson recalled.

At one point Wilson had to tell Woodham to sit down because he kept getting up and pacing the floor of the interview room.

"He was wanting to control the situation and be intimidating and I'm not intimidated by a sixteen-year-old boy, so I told him to sit down and he immediately acquiesced," Wilson said. "In my opinion, Luke was a very angry, troubled young man who thought he had made a glorious statement, philosophically wise or whatever."

Wilson insists to this day he heard no remorse or sense of sorrow from Woodham.

Tearful students left stuffed animals, roses, candles and notes beside a campus sign at the high school entrance to mourn their two dead classmates. Others left gifts against the Pearl High sign just off U.S. 80. Stephanie Ware, a sophomore, was weeping as she explained, "I told Lydia that she was in my prayers and thoughts and that God was with her."

Others like Pearl senior April Evans, a friend of Christy Menefee, said they'd also be praying for Luke Woodham. "I know he had to be really, really hurt inside to do this," she said.

On Barrow Street, Mary Anne Woodham's neighbor Merrell Jolly talked to a Pearl Police Department investigator as he walked up the Woodhams' driveway. Jolly told the detective he should interview Grant Boyette.

"He was always in that house with Luke," Jolly informed the officer. "If anyone knew why Luke did that it would be Grant because he was over there every evening."

The investigator passed on the information to his superiors. DA John Kitchens added it to his rapidly expanding file on the group known as the "Kroth."

As Rankin County Investigator Greg Eklund explained, "We had the shooter, but we were now beginning to get some input that there may have been more out there."

Twenty

Surrounded by armed guards and wearing a bullet-resistant vest, Luke Woodham showed little emotion as he was escorted into the Pearl Municipal Court on the morning of Thursday, October 2, 1997.

Dressed in a prison jumpsuit, the teen nervously pinched at the sides of his pants as he heard the charges against him formally read—seven counts of aggravated assault and three counts of murder.

"Do you understand the charges, Mr. Woodham?" asked Judge Dewey Miller.

"Yes, sir," replied Luke in a soft voice. It was one of the first times in his life he'd ever been addressed as "Mister."

Attorney Richard Wilson, who'd been seconded in the hours following Woodham's arrest, asked if his client could undergo a mental evaluation.

Judge Miller said he lacked the authority to grant the request. Wilson asked for a bond, but Miller denied that request as well.

"For his good and the good of society, I would refuse a bond to be set at this time," the judge told the court.

At the back of the courtroom, Pearl Mayor Jimmy Foster, a former school board member, and a group of Pearl school officials, including District Superintendent Bill Dodson, sat watching the pupil whom students described as intelligent but unpopular.

"I have not met the young man. I wanted to see who we're dealing with here," explained Dodson.

Outside the court, Pearl High substitute teacher Chip Smith called for the death penalty to be brought against Woodham.

"He ought to be hung for what he did. He killed three people. I saw him do it."

But, as Rankin County District Attorney John Kitchens told the court hearing, the state could not charge Woodham with capital murder, which could result in the death penalty or life imprisonment. A prosecutor could only seek the death penalty in certain circumstances, Kitchens explained—for example, if a person killed someone while committing a robbery or if a person murdered a law-enforcement officer.

If Woodham were indicted and found guilty, he would face life in prison for each slaying and a maximum twenty-year sentence on each aggravated assault charge.

"In the past we have requested that the legislature include multiple killings as one eligible for the death penalty," said Kitchens. "Perhaps now, the majority will listen and act accordingly."

As Luke Woodham left the courtroom, he paused and gazed out into a crowd of onlookers. He seemed perplexed by all the attention. For the first time in his young life he was somebody.

Ten minutes later, Woodham was back in his cell at the Rankin County Jail. As yet, Woodham had shown no suicidal tendencies, but deputies had placed him under a twenty-four-hour watch as a precaution.

* * *

On October 2, 1997, Kroth member Justin Sledge was suspended from Pearl High until further notice.

"It was best he was suspended," student Andy Prince, seventeen, agreed. Sledge needed to be suspended partly "for his own safety."

It seemed that school authorities were well aware of the connection between Sledge and Woodham—especially since he had been passed a note by the gunman just before he started his shooting rampage.

That same day, an incident occurred in a neighboring school that sparked alarm bells across the state of Mississippi. A fifteen-year-old student at the Northwest Rankin Attendance Center—just five miles from Pearl—was found to have three guns in the trunk of his car when he drove onto the school campus.

Anthony McWilliams, of Bristol Way, in nearby Brandon, was found to be armed with a .22-caliber rifle, a 7.62-caliber assault rifle, and a BB pistol, following a phone tip to police from another student.

McWilliams claimed he'd forgotten he had the weapons in his trunk, but following so soon after the Pearl rampage, it was seen as another chilling incident that convinced parents that maybe their children weren't so safe at school after all.

DA John Kitchens and his highly trained team of investigators continued examining every aspect of Luke Woodham's life for clues as to why he'd committed such appalling crimes.

As investigator Greg Eklund explained: "You gotta

establish if they're bed wetters, fire starters, cruel to animals. They are the three big ones."

Luke Woodham certainly qualified on two out of three. However, what surprised investigators was that there was absolutely no sign of drug use among Woodham or his peers. And, almost as unusual, Woodham himself did not even own a computer, so there was no question of an Internet conspiracy.

Investigator Eklund and his colleagues examined the suspect's general demeanor, along with his grades at school.

"If he's an introvert, we know that's more typical of this kind of perpetrator," Eklund said.

Investigators even closely examined the type of music Woodham listened to in case the lyrics of his favorite songs could have deadened his emotions, as had been the case in the past with other teenagers.

"If there's a drop in grades, we want to find out who this kid is spending too much time with," Eklund said.

They already had a good idea whom Woodham had been hanging out with, but they wanted to catch them off their guard. Those involved wouldn't be going anywhere fast.

DA John Kitchens's frustration about not being able to seek the death penalty against Woodham sparked an understandable outcry from those who felt the accused teen killer should pay the ultimate price for the crimes he had committed.

The *Jackson Clarion-Ledger* summed up the situation in its editorial column that week:

"Mississippians must hope and pray that such a rampage doesn't happen again, but it's clear that the laws of the state must anticipate such an atrocity—or, worse. Those who are intent on mass murder must be allowed the death penalty. Lawmakers should remember the Pearl rampage when they meet in January. The 1998 legislature should amend state law to allow prosecutors to call for and judges to impose the ultimate penalty for those who inflict such grievous harm."

The lynch mob was already out to hang Luke Woodham and he hadn't yet been found guilty in a court of law.

Thursday night, October 2, Woodham's friend and fellow group member Justin Sledge decided to publicly share his feelings about Luke and the Pearl High shootings.

He went to a candle-lit gathering in Pearl in memory of the victims and tried to address the audience.

Sledge, sixteen, delivered a disruptive, rambling monologue after telling students about the note written by Luke just before the atrocity. He told the crowd of four hundred that Woodham went mad because of society.

"Things have to change. My friend did this under my nose. He went mad because of society. We, as a society, must change," said Sledge.

Sledge hinted the violence might not yet be over. He referred to an entry in Woodham's manifesto that talked of "when you are through." It seemed to be a possible reference to further acts and it sent a shiver through the increasingly hostile crowd.

At the vigil, a number of students, gathered near a flag placed at half-mast, sobbed as they listened to

180   *Jon Bellini*

Sledge's emotionally charged address about his friend.
A few people in the crowd tried to urge Sledge to continue, but most were thankful when he was told to
leave just before 10 P.M.

The high school principal had been about to call
the police to get him removed when he finally left.

"I think he had no business justifying what Luke
did," said Brand Hoffa, an eighteen-year-old high
school student from nearby Brandon.

One freshman, Curtis Jones, fourteen, said Sledge
"was scaring people."

John Kitchens was given details of Sledge's outburst.
He believed that Sledge's words might well work
against him at some future date. Kitchens added a report of Sledge's speech to the mounting file on the
case.

Just because Sledge had made a copy of one page
of Woodham's notes and turned it over to police didn't
mean he was above suspicion. What Sledge hadn't
mentioned at the gathering was that at the end of the
manifesto, Woodham had written, "Grant, see you in
the holding cell!"

Sledge also appeared that Thursday on the nationally syndicated *Hard Copy* tabloid television show, and
the Jackson-based WLBT-Channel 3.

A special emergency meeting of the Pearl School
Board was held Thursday, too. More than 120 parents, students, teachers, and concerned citizens met
with school leaders to discuss the tragedy. At the
Pearl School District's central office, faculty hugged
each other before sitting down to talk. Employees
wore navy blue and gold ribbons in memory of the
slain students.

There was still some genuine sympathy for Luke

Woodham, and other teens who might be intellectually gifted, from a broken home, overweight, or chided by their peers.

"I know a lot of people here probably hate Luke Woodham today," said Pearl High parent Janice Franklin. "But he was a student whose intellect was not appreciated, his family life was not going well, and he'd reached a breaking point."

Franklin was convinced that children such as Woodham and her own daughter Ashley Evins had been targeted by school bullies. Another parent in the crowd stood up and echoed Franklin's sentiments, but most were still so outraged by the shootings that it was difficult to empathize with a seemingly cold-blooded killer.

Rumors were rife in Pearl about the killings being connected to some form of devil worship. Much of the gossip and innuendo was making life difficult for DA John Kitchens and his team of investigators. One rumor stemmed from a Pearl police officer picking up his daughter from Pearl Junior High in a department cruiser, as was policy in Pearl. Within minutes, a story was whipping around the school system that a child had been arrested in connection with the Pearl High shootings.

Mississippi Governor Kirk Fordice summed up the outpouring of grief about the atrocity when he told newsmen, "While this terrible tragedy happened in one community, it strikes at the hearts of every community and every parent in our state. This was a horrific act of violence, and my thoughts and prayers are with the victims and their families."

Twenty-one

Two days after the high school shootings, Grant Boyette telephoned his longtime friend Rick Brown, now a Bible student in North Carolina. Brown later claimed that Boyette admitted in the conversation that Woodham told him about plans to cause murder and mayhem at the high school.

"He [Boyette] said Luke had said that several times, but he didn't take him seriously," Brown said.

What Boyette didn't tell his friend Brown was that he'd just been interviewed by two police investigators about his friendship with Luke Woodham.

A few hours after that phone conversation, Grant Boyette withdrew from his course at Hinds Community College without explanation.

"He had no outstanding fees in the business office. He had no overdue library fees," college vice president Jimmy C. Smith said. "He just left."

The significance of his sudden departure would only later be realized.

When investigators told John Kitchens about a number of Satanic-style posters found in Woodham's bedroom, he became even more convinced that this group of students could really have been involved in planning the rampage. He decided to delve more deeply into the background of the killer and the other members of the group. It was going to be a slow process, he warned city officials keen that any new arrests be made as quickly as possible.

Kitchens already knew that many of the grieving students from Pearl High were giving counselors descriptions of cultlike activities involving the known group of six students. They talked about the shadowy coterie of teens involved with killer Luke Woodham. As the students came forward, their information was examined and carefully double-checked.

At the Crossgate Veterinary Clinic where Luke's friend Wes Brownell worked as a kennel assistant, bathing and cleaning up after cats and dogs, owner Dr. Jim Anderson noticed that he was especially upset after the Pearl shooting.

"It scared him to death. He was real scared and real upset," Anderson later recalled.

Other students and faculty in the tri-county area surrounding Pearl returned to classes Thursday, the day after the tragedy. Counselors were made available to all students, but it seemed that many preferred to talk to their friends or teachers about the horrific shooting. In schools for younger children, teachers did not give details of the shootings, but open discussions were held about safety at school.

Over at nearby Brandon High School, Principal George Gilreath encouraged his students to start a collection for a tree to be planted or some kind of memorial to the students killed and injured.

Woodham's murderous rampage prompted an outpouring of donations and other assistance. A special bank account set up in memory of the two slain students attracted more than $1,000 within a few hours of the shooting. Gifts ranged from $5 to $140. It was agreed that the funds should be used to help schools throughout Pearl purchase new security equipment, to set up a memorial for Lydia Dew and Christina Menefee, and to help cover the victims' families' medical expenses.

The Ott and Lee Funeral Home in nearby Brandon donated almost $3,000 of funeral expenses to cover the cost of Lydia Dew's service on the Friday after the shooting. Other funds raised locally paid out $4,000 for a casket and vault. At the Baldwin-Lee Funeral Home in Pearl, similar arrangements were made for the funeral service for Christina Menefee.

Funeral director Ralph Raymond summed up the situation perfectly. "This is a community need. We felt like we could donate the services," he said. "We have gone through this before. We had the Rankin County tornado a few years back. There were ten deaths. We handled seven of the ten."

Across the world, the Pearl High School shooting was given big coverage. Media organizations ranging from NBC's *Today Show*, CBS's *This Morning* and ABC's *Good Morning, America* to *Time* magazine, the *New York Times*, and London's *Daily Express* swamped Pearl in the aftermath of the atrocity.

Courageous Assistant Principal Joel Myrick described the two young victims on NBC's *Today* program. "They were two sweet little girls."

Many lauded Myrick as a hero. "What he did was a noble act," said Bruce Merchant, the Pearl Pirates football coach. "He definitely saved other lives."

Pearl Mayor Jimmy Foster said Myrick reacted well to a crisis situation. "It worked out. I'm glad he was here and had the gun in the truck."

After watching Myrick on the *Today* program, sophomore Jason Yarbo, sixteen, told one newsman: "I feel he did what he could to protect the students and staff."

Within hours of the *Today* program, Myrick was back at work with other staffers comforting students at the high school. The rampage haunted many of the youngsters. Sophomore Melissa Jenkins, sixteen, was a good example.

"I've had sleepless nights. I hear gunshots in my sleep," she said nervously.

On the Friday, October 3, Luke Woodham was given his first psychiatric examination. Psychiatrist Dr. Reb McMichael quickly got to what he believed was the core of Woodham's mentality.

"He said he hated the world," McMichael recalled. "He saw that as a means to getting to an end. The end wasn't Satan worship. He saw that as a way of getting revenge."

The funerals of both high school victims, Christina Menefee and Lydia Dew, were held just two hours apart on Friday, October 3.

At the service for Dew at the Ott and Lee Funeral Home, the Reverend David Warren spoke of the vibrant teenager whose life ended violently without warning.

"Lydia was a kind and friendly person, just a bubbly person," said Warren of the teen, whom neighbors remembered as the girl who would just pick up a rake and start to clean up their yards.

Students at the service remembered her as one who would lift their spirits and offer a hug or a helping hand.

As he consoled sobbing students, Warren said: "She's got a jumpstart on us. She's already in the presence of the Lord . . . she had a date with God before she had a date with death."

After the funeral, many of Dew's friends were not prepared to forgive their classmate Luke Woodham for killing their friend.

"Lydia was a very dear friend of mine. The person who did this needs to rot in hell. He is sick," said one student outside the funeral home.

Just a few miles away at the Baldwin-Lee Funeral Home, tearful students, school and community leaders attended the service for Christina Menefee.

Menefee, an honors student who excelled in the ROTC program, was buried in her uniform, in an American flag-shrouded casket.

Her father, Bob Menefee, had never in his life had to make funeral arrangements—and now he was doing it for his sixteen-year-old daughter.

Charles Sandler, Christy's Junior ROTC naval science instructor at Pearl High, read a statement from Menefee's father describing her as "my special angel.

Christina was a beacon in the darkest night. She was the light of my life."

Christy Menefee was buried at the Glenwood Memorial Park in Richland in a space donated free of charge. At least two monument companies in the area offered to donate markers for the two bereaved families.

At the Menefee family home in Pearl, Christy's father put a photo of his beloved daughter in every room and wouldn't touch any other reminders of her, such as her toothbrush and favorite cologne.

Talking about his loss was obviously difficult. As he explained at the time: "I go from one extreme to the other, from missing her and sorrow and grief and anger. I go back and forth every day."

And every time he looked out at the backyard he could see Christy's beloved rose garden.

Bob Menefee also refused to believe that his daughter's doomed friendship with Luke Woodham was anything more than a few chaperoned dates over a brief period. "I believe he was a lot more serious about my daughter than she was about him," said Menefee.

Following the two funerals on Friday more than seven hundred Pearl High students returned for counseling sessions on the school campus. Many of them knelt at the high school sign on Pirate Cove as a mark of respect for their dead and injured classmates.

An army of pastors and area counselors were in constant attendance and they expected to return many times to the campus over the following weeks and months.

As Pearl High history teacher David Sansing, Jr., explained, "We are with these kids every day. They are part of our lives and ingrained in our hearts, minds, and souls. We will see them as much as the parents do. They are our family."

Sansing encouraged students to attend counseling sessions at Pearl High, but he admitted: "We will all feel the sadness for the rest of our lives."

Pearl High School staff were particularly concerned that students shouldn't go through the grieving process alone.

Sansing's advice was, "Talk it over with other kids, teachers, and family members. Cry if you have to cry."

Jeff Canon, director of the Pearl Pirates marching band, praised the counseling efforts. "It's helped me to talk about it," he said. "The students just don't need to be afraid. We'll get through this."

Luke Woodham's onetime friend Wes Brownell seemed very distracted during a counseling session at the high school that same Friday following the shootings.

"He was the only one who didn't say anything," recalled Jeff Hill of New Life Christian Fellowship in Brandon. Hill was there to assist a teacher speaking with students in the wake of the tragedy.

What particularly struck Hill was Brownell's complete blankness about the high school killings. It greatly bothered the preacher.

While Assistant Principal Joel Myrick was hailed a hero in many quarters for disarming Woodham, questions were asked as to why he kept a gun in his truck in the school parking lot.

State law clearly said that no person—adult or student—could have a gun in his or her possession on a school campus. However, the law made an exception for adults—not students—who kept guns in their vehicles on campus and didn't brandish them in a threatening manner.

Myrick stated he had the unloaded gun in his truck's glove compartment because he'd traveled upcountry over the previous weekend to visit family members. He said it was perfectly normal for him to take the gun with him.

"A million things were going through my mind, but I knew I could not take him bare-handed," he explained. "I ran to my truck and retrieved my .45 automatic and loaded it. It had to be done."

Myrick said he would have fired the gun if he had needed to, "or I would not have drawn it."

One local law expert said that the school district would have been legally liable if a student had discovered Myrick's weapon and used it.

On Friday, October 3, the *Clarion-Ledger* ran numerous articles about the atrocity underneath a banner headline that read ALLEGED GUNMAN DESCRIBED AS "INTELLIGENT," "PICKED ON." Some of Luke's so-called buddies played a starring role in these articles.

Most prominent among them was Grant Boyette, who was described as someone who "sometimes played video games with Woodham." Boyette called his young friend "a reader, very intelligent." Woodham "loved philosophy," added Boyette. He even told newsmen he'd asked himself a thousand times why Woodham hadn't talked to him about whatever had been troubling him.

Boyette also said he believed Woodham intended for

him to have the journals Woodham handed to Justin Sledge prior to the shootings. Boyette openly admitted he'd already been interviewed by police and feared that Sledge would be arrested. He described himself as a close friend who often offered Woodham advice.

Boyette criticized Sledge for his behavior at the candle-lit vigil. "That ain't right. It ain't right to go there and do all that," said Boyette. "I think that a lot of people have been angry at the Pearl Police Department because of Justin, but I think they've done the right thing. And I think there's no way you can justify what Luke did. I was considered by him to be his best friend, and still what he did was wrong."

Boyette even said he'd asked himself a thousand times why Woodham hadn't asked him for help. "No one else took care of him. When he cried, I held him. When he was in trouble, I helped him when no one else did. I just didn't know this was going to happen. No one could know this was going to happen."

Another of Woodham's friends to be interviewed by the media was Justin Sledge. He told several press outlets he wanted to explain Woodham's actions. He insisted the shootings had been oversimplified and once again read from the one-page "manifesto" Woodham had given to him just before the atrocity.

Sledge insisted Woodham's killing spree had not been caused by a "boyfriend-girlfriend thing." He said that Woodham's parents' divorce was not a relevant factor, either.

"The reason I believe that he [Woodham] did it was because society as a whole put down the thinkers and the true geniuses of the world and replaced them with men whose strength is physical strength and physical abilities," said Sledge.

Later that same day, he told one Jackson TV station that, "Luke was tired of so-called society dealing the thinkers, the learners, a bad hand while watching Johnny football player get the glory when in actuality he does nothing."

Police interviewed another member of the Kroth, Wes Brownell.

One of Brownell's best friends, Josh Maxey, insisted that Brownell was not in any way involved with the group. "We went to movies, went to the mall looking for chicks. We're normal teenagers. We have normal fun," said Maxey. "That group wasn't his kinda scene."

DA John Kitchens obviously didn't agree. His investigation was gaining momentum. Over the weekend following the tragedy, he urged investigators to step up a gear in their inquiries.

Other Pearl High students visited in Pearl on the Saturday and Sunday painted a picture of Luke Woodham as being heavily under the spell of the older boys in the group, especially Grant Boyette. One of Luke's classmates at school told detectives how the older, tougher set of kids had boasted of their Satanic links. Investigators uncovered evidence that suggested the teens had been planning "a devastating act" for many months. Boyette was identified as the "father" of the so-called "Kroth," and Woodham was tagged as the "assassin" of the group.

Rankin County Investigator Greg Eklund explained: "We'd got statements from several of the other kids in the school. They were linking this small group that Luke spoke with every day. We needed to know if Luke had said anything to them before the shootings. That would then be a precursor of what was going to happen. But as the investigation continued, it became very clear that not only did he confide in these people, but he told them everything first. There had even been talk about taking control of the school and people dying."

The body of the one victim no one seemed concerned about was released by the Rankin County Medical Examiner's Office. Mary Anne Woodham was to be buried some miles from Pearl in a secluded site, attended by just a handful of relatives and friends, including her son John. Luke Woodham was not invited.

Twenty-two

Pearl High students braced themselves for an emotional return to school on Monday, October 6, just five days after the fatal shootings. Police officers and pastors mingled with the students, and by ten A.M. only a hundred members of the 1,039-student campus were still absent—not much more than on a normal Monday.

There were only a few regular classes held that day. Most of the time students and teachers discussed the events and tried to come to terms with the tragedy. More than 300 of the students had skipped the counseling classes held the previous Friday. Many admitted they were very scared about going back to the scene of the tragedy.

Seven PPD officers, including a number who had children of their own at the school, kept a low profile as a solemn procession of students made their way through the commons where Luke Woodham had killed and injured his nine victims.

A couple of hours later, a PPD detective entered an English class at the high school and asked to speak to student Wes Brownell. Brownell raised his hand and then walked outside with the cop, who then slapped cuffs on the teenager and took him to a waiting police cruiser.

Brownell later claimed that on the ride to the Pearl police station, two uniformed officers tried to intimidate him by telling him the inmates at the state penitentiary would take special care of him because he was so young.

"It was scare tactics," Brownell later insisted. But whatever his bravado at the time, he was worried.

Monday evening, one of Woodham's intended targets, athlete Kyle Foster, was playing the tough guy once again in a football game against school rivals Northwest Rankin. Some were surprised that the game went ahead, but there was an overriding feeling that things at Pearl should get back to normal as quickly as possible.

"Otherwise we ain't ever gonna recover from this awful crime," explained one parent at the game.

Kyle's father, Pearl Mayor Jimmy Foster, watched proudly as his son put in a sterling performance as tight end for the Pearl Pirates. Foster told newsmen proudly: "He [Kyle] made some good hits last night. He's taking out his frustrations."

Many wondered if Luke Woodham had a similar outlet before he ruined his life and that of so many others forever.

DA John Kitchens and his team reassessed on Monday night how their investigation was progressing. It was already clear from the teens interviewed so far that Woodham informed others of his plan and some of them clearly had implied that it was all part of a bigger, more destructive scheme.

Kitchens decided to order the arrest of those other teens who'd become so close to the main perpetrator, Luke Woodham. Within hours they were brought to the Rankin County Sheriff's Department in Brandon. Each posed for mugshots. The looks on their faces seemed to provide some sort of insight into their psyches. They all had steely, grim expressions.

Tuesday, October 7, was the day Pearl was almost brought to its knees. Justin Sledge, sixteen, Daniel "Lucas" Thompson, sixteen, Wesley Brownell, seventeen, Donald P. Brooks II, seventeen, and Delbert Alan Shaw, eighteen, were accused of conspiracy to murder other students at the high school.

Marshall "Grant" Boyette, eighteen, had also been arrested on charges of conspiracy to commit murder.

Boyette and Brooks were charged with a second count of conspiracy to commit murder against Brooks's father, Donald Brooks, Sr., a Pearl firefighter. All were being held in the Rankin County Detention Center on one-million-dollar bond per count. If found guilty, they faced a maximum penalty of life in prison.

All pleaded innocent in the Rankin County Circuit Court that afternoon. Afterward, all were taken off to separate cells in the Rankin County Jail.

The revelation that others may have been involved in the Pearl High rampage sent the city into shock.

"It was bad enough when we believed that it was a tragic, isolated incident," said Pearl official Ron Morgan. "But if this is not an isolated incident, then what was it? How far does it reach?"

Others who thought the healing process was starting to take hold in the city got a rude awakening. Everyone agreed it was scary to think that a group of teens might have been planning an atrocity in their midst.

Pearl was supposed to be a place where people felt safe all the time. Now all that had been ruined—possibly forever.

Ironically, all this murder and mayhem may have been born out of the baseball program, softball program, soccer, and football—all run by parents who had indirectly excluded the Luke Woodhams of this world.

June Goodin, the mother of one defendant, Delbert Alan Shaw, waited with family members at the Rankin County Jail after her son and the five others were returned to their cells after arraignment. She insisted that her son had lived with her in Louisville, a town ninety miles northeast of Pearl, for the previous two weeks and was not even in Pearl when the shootings happened.

"He knew all those children who were shot and was just devastated," said Goodin. "I drove him back down for the funerals, and he wanted to stay in Pearl and finish his education."

Lawyers for three of the accused teens had already claimed they'd ended their relationship with Woodham long before the Pearl shootings. Kitchens knew that would prove a tough mitigating circumstance to fight when their cases came to court.

Kitchens had unraveled a bizarre web that firmly suggested Luke Woodham was not acting alone when he blasted those two innocent high school students to death.

Shortly after the arrest of the six teens, Kitchens said, "The conduct that has been uncovered in the investigation that has been ongoing since Wednesday goes so far beyond right and wrong it's tragic."

Referring to the arrest of Woodham's six alleged co-conspirators, Kitchens said, "The conduct engaged by those charged is so anti-Christian and anti-society that it is revolting."

Emotional words that would send waves of horror and revulsion through the community where blue ribbons still hung outside homes on virtually every city street in memorial to the slain girls.

On October 9, two days after the teens were arrested, Donnie Brooks was lying on the bed in his cell at the Rankin County Detention Center when an officer appeared and opened the cell door.

Brooks thought to himself: "What does he want this time?"

"Get your things together," barked the guard without elaborating.

Unable to carry everything he needed, a cellmate advised Brooks to put all his belongings in a blanket and use it like a sack.

"You're probably being moved to another cell," suggested the cellmate.

Brooks was then told to complete his housekeeping duties before a guard escorted him to the jail entrance, where his attorney, James Bell, stood waiting.

One of the jailers shoved a piece of paper toward Brooks and told him to sign it. That done, the distinctive *buzz-pop* of the electronic lock of the jail's inner door could be heard, and across the threshold, the outer door lock sprang open. As Brooks stepped into the cold early morning air, he saw the waiting entourage of his family.

"It was like, 'What's going on here?' I didn't say it, but I was thinking that in the back of my mind," Brooks later said.

Brooks walked out the door and the next thing he knew his dad, best friend, and his mother were waiting.

"It was like, 'Oh, I'm out.' I still didn't know if I was going to have to go back."

Donnie Brooks was released on his own recognizance and told newsmen, "It was a bunch of mixed emotions. It was shock, surprise, happiness, joy. I can't even name them all."

Despite the charges against his son that included conspiring to kill him, Brooks's father said: "I never doubted my son's love for me. Never."

Brooks and his father held an impromptu press conference that ended abruptly at two-thirty P.M. when Rankin County Assistant District Attorney Jim Kelly called to tell Brooks's attorney James Bell that there was no immediate chance of the charges against his client being dropped, as Bell had predicted.

Donnie Brooks, a senior, was told that he would not be welcome back at Pearl High.

"Before Mr. Brooks would be allowed to return to school on any basis, we will need to sit down with him, his family and his lawyer to determine the most appropriate educational course for him," Pearl School Board Attorney Skip Jernigan said.

Donnie Brooks studied at home, went to movies a couple of times with his sister Kim, and to the store occasionally with his parents. But there were genuine fears that he and the other youths could be in danger if they were seen out and about frequently.

Brooks relied heavily on one close friend and he was told that unless things changed drastically, he would be holding his prom and graduation ceremony at the family home in Pearl.

Donnie Brooks's attorney claimed his release was the first step in getting the charges against his client dropped. He was convinced Brooks's case would be thrown out because he had evidence he had told authorities what was happening four months before the shootings.

Justin Sledge and Lucas Thompson were moved from the Rankin County Jail to a youth holding center, suggesting they wouldn't be prosecuted as adults. The move must have come as a relief to the two teens. If their cases were heard in the Youth Court, they would only face serving time in a training school if found guilty.

At Pearl High, many students closed ranks after the arrest of the six conspiracy suspects.

"It sorta came home to us just how crazy this whole thing was," one student said. "How could they seriously have hoped to get away with it?"

Others were plain scared about stating anything publicly about the accused teens. Pearl wasn't a big city by any means. Parents, friends, and enemies of the suspects were not hard to bump into any morning or afternoon.

Rankin County Coroner Jimmy Roberts refused to publicly release results of the autopsies on all three victims. He would only confirm that Mary Anne Wood-ham had been stabbed to death.

Neither Pearl Police Chief Bill Slade nor DA John Kitchens would explain the coroner's decision. Many speculated that the method and way the victims died might become crucial evidence at a trial.

Authorities were also not publicly forthcoming about any of the backgrounds of the accused teens. They even refused to say whether specific students had been targeted to be killed or to confirm any connection between Woodham and the six others. Slade and Kitchens also wouldn't comment on rumors that the students were involved in a cult or if any further arrests could be expected. Perhaps most significantly, the two lawmen refused to say whether any adults were involved in the alleged conspiracy.

The days following the teens' first court appearance, Pearl High School officials banned members of the news media from the campus amid accusations of intrusive behavior. It had been just a week since the rampage. Dozens of news reporters, photographers, and television crews from around the country were asked to leave the school.

Students and teachers accused the media of whipping up a frenzy of fear by reporting many of the wild rumors flying around Pearl following the rampage. One parent faxed a note to Pearl Schools Superintendent Bill Dodson pleading, "Stop the continued violation of our Pearl High students! Protect them from the media."

* * *

On the afternoon of Wednesday, October 8, the Pearl Police Department received a copy of the statement made by Donnie Brooks four months before the high school rampage.

Chief Bill Slade knew what the implications of the statement were—if someone had acted upon the information at the time, then the deaths of three people could have been avoided.

Slade knew this wouldn't be the last he would hear about Brooks's statement, but for the moment, investigators studied it before handing it over to DA John Kitchens, who accepted that it would not help their case against Brooks.

That same Wednesday, some Pearl High students suffered what can only be described as a bizarre delayed reaction to the trauma of the Woodham rampage. Almost 200 students skipped classes and another 40 signed out early. It was considerably more than at the start of the week and led many to believe that counseling was not necessarily the instant solution.

"These kids have been in a war. They are too young for it," explained Assistant Principal Joel Myrick.

That morning former Pearl student Troy Parker had turned up at the campus dressed in black clothing, a black trench coat, and sporting a skinhead haircut. Staff and students were so alarmed that they ordered him to leave the campus.

Meanwhile, school officials refuted persistent rumors that many students would be transferring out of the school. But Pearl sophomore Amanda Mallette, fifteen, summed up many of the students' feelings when she said: "It scares me with all the people arrested.

I'm scared there are more people not found out about yet."

Two days after Grant Boyette was indicted on charges of accessory to murder before the fact, investigators obtained a warrant to search his family's neat home on Summit Ridge Road, in nearby Brandon. Writings, drawings, pictures, computer games, notes, notebooks, letters, books, and computer disks were removed by police.

At the Rankin County Jail, Luke Woodham told his court-appointed lawyer Richard H. Wilson that he no longer required the services of a lawyer. For the moment, Woodham told his guards, he was going to defend himself.

At eight P.M. on Friday, October 10, Wes Brownell was released on $50,000 bond after a day of legal wrangling. His attorney Wayne Milner said his client should never have been arrested and charged in the first place. He insisted, "I'm not an apologetic person for the horrible crimes that happened at Pearl High. But it's also a horrible tragedy to round up this young man at school and keep him here in jail."

Josh Maxey said, "It's really upsetting to know you might go to jail for something you didn't do. He's only seventeen. That's a pretty disturbing thing. I don't think you'll find anyone that thinks Wes is guilty except maybe the DA."

Delbert Alan Shaw, eighteen, was also released on $3,000 bond on October 11. His attorney, John Colette, said he believed his client was less culpable than some of the others accused of murder conspiracy and Colette predicted that he would eventually work out a deal with prosecutors.

DA John Kitchens made it plain that Rankin County had no plans to allow bail for Grant Boyette, referred to as the mastermind of the group. No bail for Luke Woodham was already a foregone conclusion.

Sledge and Thompson remained at the nearby youth detention center. It was unclear whether they could also shortly be given their liberty.

The notion of a dime-store führer like Grant Boyette inspiring apostles of terror, along with rumors of Satanism, continued to send ripples through the community of Pearl. DA John Kitchens soon claimed to have uncovered even more details of the so-called Satanic coven. Evidence came from three sources: the other alleged conspirators who'd identified Boyette as their leader, neighbors, and friends.

One of the star witnesses would be Rick Brown, the former Pearl High pupil training to be a preacher. Not only did he tell investigators that Boyette had avidly followed the works of Adolf Hitler, admiring the way he manipulated people, but he also spoke in detail about the telephone conversation he had had with Boyette after the high school killings.

Brown said Boyette had telephoned him two days after the rampage and told him how he [Boyette] had talked to Woodham the night before he'd killed his mother and the following morning—the time when, prosecutors alleged, Woodham committed the first of three murders.

* * *

The family of Lydia Dew was having to face up to the awful realization that Lydia had lost her life because she was an innocent bystander.

"Lydia was not a target. She wasn't involved in anything like this. She wasn't part of this," her mother, Kaye Long, told reporters.

Kaye Long's other daughter, Lea Ann Dew, echoed the feelings of many in Pearl when she said, "I'm scared. I'm scared of everything. I don't know who else was in this group and if there are any left."

Investigators continued sifting through every minute piece of forensic evidence because they suspected that some of the group might have been present in the Woodham house when Luke murdered his mother. That was one of the main reasons why DA Kitchens and the police were so reluctant to publicly talk about the case. Although they had arrested all their suspects, it was far from an airtight case and Kitchens didn't want to risk playing into the defense's hands.

As part of the in-depth investigation, six of the group had to provide DNA samples so that checks could be made to see if they had left any evidence inside the Woodham house.

The DNA tests later confirmed that none of the six teens were with Woodham that morning, but it had been a measure of how concerned investigators were that they went to the trouble of performing the DNA tests.

Just over a week after the high school shootings, Pearl Mayor Jimmy Foster revealed that his son was not the only target in Luke Woodham's sights. He claimed that another "prominent city official's child" was on Woodham's death list and that virtually everyone at the school knew who that person was.

Foster, a former local police chief, said the family of the intended victim had asked for anonymity, but he was prepared to talk openly about his own son's situation after working more than two decades in local law enforcement.

"This whole situation has made me sick to my stomach, and I've seen a lot of things in twenty-three years of law enforcement. Wednesday morning, I punted my mayoral football and went back into law enforcement."

Foster said he believed his own son Kyle had been targeted by Woodham because the shooting would have created a lot of exposure. He also claimed he'd heard "unsubstantiated" rumors that others involved with Woodham wanted to "finish off the job."

Pearl remained a hotbed of rumor and counterrumor, but most students dismissed the mayor's claims. They believed that Woodham's incarceration would bring the killing spree to an end.

A group from the local pentecostal church in Pearl displayed a banner that read PRAYER BACK IN THE SCHOOLS outside the high school campus and later at city hall.

Diane Rayborn, a fifteen-year-old sophomore, hoped the message would be seen by the audience of the nationally syndicated *Geraldo Rivera Show* that was in town to tape interviews with survivors.

"If we'd had a prayer in school, it would never have happened," Rayborn said. "He [God] showed what it's like when He's not in the picture. He wants to be in our school."

The Rivera team built itself a set in front of Pearl City Hall and featured Kaye Long, mother of victim Lydia Dew, as well as several other guests from within the community.

Long sat in a chair, with a picture of her daughter, next to one of Dew's friends and others directly affected by the rampage.

As host Rivera began talking to Long through an earpiece microphone from New York City, Long began sobbing and repeated several times she did not want to talk on the show. After a few seconds, she got up and walked off the set.

Other guests included Chief Bill Slade, Mayor Jimmy Foster, and wounded student Deepika Dhawan. Woodham had agreed to legal assistance, and his new defense attorneys, Leslie Roussell and Eric Tiebauer, did not try to stop Dhawan. There was a feeling that she'd suffered enough already.

A couple of days later, while attending a church service with his mother, Linda, Wes Brownell was approached by a television reporter. As the teenager left the service, the journalist shoved a microphone in his face and asked Brownell if he knew he wasn't welcome at the church.

Brownell looked stunned. He later claimed the reporter was wrong. "People at church were real supportive. They knew it wasn't true," he later said. Brownell never elaborated on what he was referring to.

Christy Menefee's mother, Sheila Jeffers, watched countless television shows about the tragedy.

"I'm not going to say I want Christy avenged. That would be cruel. I would like to see justice done. This boy killed my daughter, and he's with this group of children who have no business in Satanic cults. What's going on in this world?"

Virtually nothing had been seen or heard of Luke's father, John P. Woodham II. Attorneys referred to him as Woodham's "legal guardian," although he had not participated in any of the legal decisions in the aftermath of the Pearl High shootings.

In any case, Woodham had been charged as an adult so he didn't even need a guardian as his case moved through the courts. But his father's absence disturbed many in the community who suspected that with the right type of parental involvement, Luke Woodham might never have turned into a mass killer.

"It tells you a lot about his life at home—and it's very sad," said one investigator.

Ten days after the tragedy, Pearl City officials had to face up to the stark reality of taking some kind of responsibility for the school shootings. Woodham's history suggested he was primed to explode. He had reached a point where committing a violent act seemed the best way to solve a problem.

Despite the shock and stunned disbelief surrounding the Pearl High shootings, most conceded there was no way school officials could have installed a foolproof system that would have tagged Woodham or any other student as a potential killer. But there were already a number of unanswered questions that seemed to suggest the entire tragedy could have been avoided:

1. Why was no action taken after Donnie Brooks gave his statement to authorities four months before the atrocity?

2. Why wasn't the dysfunctional state of Luke Woodham's home life the subject of some kind of social services inquiry long before the shootings?

3. Why weren't Luke Woodham's manifesto and disturbing classroom exercises back from 1995 studied more closely and acted upon?

Not surprisingly there were already rumors in Pearl that Christy Menefee's family was contemplating a wrongful death lawsuit. Lydia Dew's family seemed set to follow them. Their case was stronger than the Menefee's as Lydia had not been connected in any way to the gunman.

Pearl School Board Attorney Skip Jernigan issued a statement saying it was impossible to be culpable for Woodham's actions. "How do you prevent something that you don't know about?" Jernigan said. "We had no evidence that this would take place, no way to see it could take place. Before you have a duty, you have to know an event is foreseeable."

On Monday, October 13, Pearl Police Chief Bill Slade held a brief press conference in advance of the first preliminary court hearing involving the six teens charged with conspiracy linked to the high school shootings.

The issue of whether anyone knew what Woodham was planning to do was only just beginning to gain momentum. And the questions surrounding Donnie Brooks's interview with authorities four months before the shootings were proving a political hot potato.

Slade read out a terse two-sentence statement: "The Pearl Police Department had no knowledge of any written statement dealing with the tragedy of Pearl High School. A copy of this statement was received from a source outside the department on the afternoon of October 8 that was in no way related to the tragedy."

He refused to answer any questions.

People were starting to think it could all have been avoided.

mountain. And the question, surrounding house
... a function, with Bill's linear ... month, ...
the bondings were proving ... painted ... point ...
State read twice here been ... once par ... near ... "The
... of Police Department has no knowledge of any
... investigation dealing with the body of Jean
Hill school. A copy of this ... report was ... to
from a senior officer ... reported ... the state-
... in October, 1884 ... in no way related to the
...

He turned to answer the questions.

People were incredulous that it could all have been
missed.

Twenty-three

On Tuesday, October 14, Grant Boyette entered the Rankin County Court for a preliminary hearing. His spindly frame barely filled his orange, short-sleeved county jail jumpsuit.

The teen immediately sat down and folded his hands in his lap and didn't move them once throughout the hearing. He spoke rarely with his attorneys and seldom even looked up.

The hearing was told how Boyette was an admirer of Adolf Hitler and leader of the Kroth, the name of the accused group of conspirators.

Rankin County Sheriff's Department Investigator Greg Eklund told the court Boyette was intrigued with Hitler's ability to manipulate people, and Boyette had then convinced Woodham to go on the shooting rampage.

"He was the one who called the shots. Nobody in the group bucked Mr. Boyette," said Eklund.

He gave the court a chilling presentation of the group led by Boyette, with Woodham as his assassin. Eklund said Boyette also gave others in the group specific tasks. Under Boyette's guidance, Eklund continued, the group met at Woodham's home and plotted the "takeover" of Pearl High, a five-minute period of time in which they would execute certain students and faculty and blow up the school. They would then flee to Cuba.

Eklund quoted witnesses as saying that Boyette had told them he owned an AK-47 assault rifle and had access to other weapons and a large amount of money. Eklund said other members of the group also heard Boyette urge Woodham to end the heartache of his separation from Christina Menefee.

"On many occasions, he told Luke Woodham he should just kill her and be done with it so he won't have to see her again," Eklund told a stunned courtroom.

Eklund then told the court the plan to kill Donnie Brooks's father with the poison on the doorknobs, before relating how Boyette asserted so much power over Woodham that he (Woodham) killed his pet dog, Sparkle. Abusing the dog was, said Eklund, a tactic by Boyette to manipulate Woodham and explained the hierarchy of roles between Boyette, the "mastermind," and Woodham, "the assassin."

Boyette's longtime friend Rick Brown also testified about Boyette's interest in Hitler and Satan while in high school. Brown also told how Boyette had telephoned him two days after the rampage and told him he (Boyette) had talked to Woodham the night before he'd killed his mom and the following morning.

Brown also claimed that Boyette, Woodham, and the others in the group had first gotten together to play a game, but that "they just kept playing and kept getting deeper and deeper into it and got obsessed with it and got in over their heads."

Brown said he had no idea how involved his friend Grant Boyette intended to be in the killings and even stated that if he (Brown) was on a jury, he'd have to "let him go because there is a shadow of doubt whether or not Grant was involved to the point that he really conspired to kill somebody."

As another of Boyette's friends pointed out at the time, "Who needs enemies when you've got Rick Brown on your side?"

Brown, the softly spoken student at the Southeastern Free Will Baptist Bible College, seemed to be doing an old-fashioned demolition job on his onetime best buddy.

In his statement to the court (and later to the local media), Brown went on to say: "I never expected anything like this to happen. I didn't expect for it to go as far as it did. I certainly didn't expect Luke to be involved. Luke is a real peace-natured guy. I don't think he was capable of doing it. I still don't think he was capable of this. That's the other thing that makes me think Grant is involved. Maybe he talked him into doing it—not thinking that Luke would ever do it."

Brown spoke about how he had counseled Woodham in the teachings of God and tried to help ease his frustrations about life as an adolescent.

Brown said he thought that depictions of both Woodham and Boyette as being smart students picked on by classmates were exaggerated and he certainly didn't rate either of the teens as being frustrated geniuses.

Then Brown made his most damning statement of all to the court. "I wouldn't want him [Boyette] out with the possibility that he's the leader of some cult that's killing people. I feel like it is possible that Grant was so vengeful and full of hatred that he wanted to prove to the world that he shouldn't have been picked on all his life, that he'd been underestimated."

Brown said he would not recommend releasing

Boyette on bond and painted a dark picture of his onetime classmate, referring to him "praying to Satan for power, influence and money."

Several church members, family friends, and former teachers appeared in court to say they would not be afraid to see Boyette freed.

"He seemed to have his head screwed on pretty good," said Billy Baker, a Sunday school teacher at Crossgate Baptist Church. "He knew a good bit about scripture."

The case against Grant Boyette was starting to look very promising to DA John Kitchens. He knew that in many ways Brown's statement was like a gift from the heavens because the teen seemed to be suggesting exactly what Kitchens believed—that Boyette had masterminded everything Woodham did on October 1.

After more than four hours of detailed testimony, Rankin County Judge Kent McDaniel revoked Boyette's two-million-dollar bond.

"Grant Boyette apparently lives two very different lives," said the judge. "For those [sympathetic] people to be so utterly wrong about him proves that Mr. Boyette must have been extremely deceptive, if any of the testimony is to be believed. Those people only served the need to hold him in jail."

Pearl High sophomore Jessica Rambo, sixteen, thought she'd witnessed the ultimate horror when she saw Luke Woodham's murderous attack—until just seventeen days later. She walked out of her home on Harahan Road to see yellow crime-scene tape draped in front of the apartment block and all the memories of the school shooting came flooding back.

Two of her neighbors had died violently in a murder-suicide. So much for quiet, peace-loving Pearl. The troubles in the community seemed to be mounting.

"I don't sleep good at night. I have to take Tylenol PM," Rambo told one friend. "There are some nights when I've slept on the floor at the foot of my parents' bed."

The latest double killing left many Pearl residents wondering just why their community seemed to be falling apart at the seams.

On Wednesday, October 15, the citizens of Pearl were further rocked by the news that two of the teenagers accused of the high school murder conspiracy would face additional charges that could lead to life in prison. Grant Boyette and Justin Sledge were each indicted on two counts of accessory to murder before the fact.

Indictments presented to the grand jury stated that, from April to October 1, the two teens persuaded their close friend Luke Woodham to go into the high school and shoot and kill Christina Menefee and Lydia Dew.

Pearl City Prosecutor Jason Zebert explained that the accessory charges came about as a direct result of what investigators had uncovered in the weeks since the shootings.

"The difference is if we get together and plan a crime—that's a conspiracy," said Zebert. "If I poke and prod you along to kill someone, that's accessory before the fact."

One of the other students' attorneys, Randy Harris, said, "It could mean they [Sledge and Boyette] were just as guilty as if they went into the school themselves. For what they were indicted, that is deliberate design to murder."

Even Boyette's counsel, Ed Rainer, conceded afterward that his client and Sledge were "definitely the main targets."

Sledge, still only sixteen, was returned to adult jail from the Rankin County Youth Detention Center and held without bond. Boyette, who was older, was taken straight to the county jail.

Meanwhile, Prosecutor Zebert told reporters he didn't expect to see any new arrests. "What we're dealing with is a tragedy. Pearl is a wonderful place to live. People have to try not to be paranoid."

But more and more questions were now being asked as to whether the tragedy of Pearl High could have been avoided if Donnie Brooks's statement to authorities four months before the shootings had been acted upon.

Police Chief Bill Slade continued to insist the statement had "nothing to do with the high school," but refused to release it, claiming it was part of the evidence in the investigation into the tragedy. Slade did confirm that Brooks's statement mentioned "the Kroth," but said that nothing was done about it because it didn't directly relate to the high school. Chief Slade repeated that he did not even learn about the existence of the statement until a week after the Pearl shootings.

Then, twenty-four hours later, in a bizarre meeting with local journalists, Slade produced the statement and conceded that the high school was mentioned once. But he still refused to identify the authorities who originally took the statement.

As one Pearl resident pointed out at the time: "It looked to many of us as if there was a hell of a lot of backpedaling going on."

Donnie Brooks's attorney, James Bell, categorically

stated his client did meet with Pearl police on June 11 and that he had clearly stated to an officer that he and other teens belonged to a group that practiced bizarre behavior.

Chief Slade insisted he had nothing to hide. "There is no cover-up here. Once everyone sees this come out in court, they'll see this was a defense attorney's tactic," said Slade. "That's what they get paid to do."

Pearl Schools Superintendent Bill Dodson once again said that neither he nor any school official was aware of the Brooks statement.

Overall, the charges against the six alleged co-conspirators in the Pearl shooting sparked a lot of confusion and panic in the community. And they made for grim reading:

LUKE WOODHAM
Three counts of murder; maximum penalty if convicted—life.
Seven counts of aggravated assault; maximum penalty—twenty years each count.
One count of conspiracy to murder students at Pearl High; maximum penalty—twenty years.
One count of conspiracy to murder Donald Brooks, Sr.; maximum penalty—twenty years.

GRANT BOYETTE
Two counts of accessory to murder before the fact; maximum penalty—life.
One count of conspiracy to murder students at Pearl High; maximum penalty—twenty years.
One count of conspiracy to murder Donald Brooks, Sr.; maximum penalty—twenty years.

JUSTIN SLEDGE

Two counts of accessory to murder before the fact; maximum penalty—life.

One count of conspiracy to murder students at Pearl High; maximum penalty—twenty years.

One count of conspiracy to murder Donald Brooks, Sr.; maximum penalty—twenty years.

DONALD BROOKS

One count of conspiracy to murder Donald Brooks, Sr.; maximum penalty—twenty years.

One count of conspiracy to murder students at Pearl High; maximum penalty—twenty years.

WESLEY BROWNELL

One count of conspiracy to murder students at Pearl High; maximum penalty—twenty years.

DELBERT "ALAN" SHAW

One count of conspiracy to murder students at Pearl High; maximum penalty—twenty years.

DANIEL LUCAS THOMPSON

Charged with conspiracy to murder; case now in Youth Court.

Not even the age-old custom of Halloween could escape the curse of Luke Woodham's appalling crimes. Thursday, October 30, 1997, became Pearl's designated day to celebrate Halloween, instead of the following day, following an order from city mayor Jimmy Foster.

Foster claimed it was because the city police did not have enough manpower to provide a safe level of security. But with the shootings still very fresh in everyone's mind, it was clear that Foster's decision was closely connected to the dreadful incidents that occurred on October 1.

The morning of Pearl's designated Halloween day,

Wes Brownell pleaded not guilty to conspiracy to murder charges relating to the high school shootings. Wearing blue jeans and a rugby-style shirt, the Pearl High junior remained quiet and stood erect throughout his appearance before Rankin County Circuit Judge Samac Richardson.

His mother, Linda Brownell, comforted her son by patting him on the shoulder and giving him words of support.

Brownell still insisted he'd ended his friendship with Luke Woodham long before the alleged conspiracy had taken place. He revealed that he'd offered to take a lie-detector test at the Pearl police station following his initial arrest. Brownell also said that he considered the two slain girl students to be friends and claimed he was as surprised as anyone when Woodham went on his shooting rampage.

His mother insisted that her son was "not Luke's good buddy." She told reporters that Brownell had distanced himself from Woodham some months before the tragedy. "I don't know what happened, but my son had enough sense to stop hanging around with him."

Many of the teens and their families realized that to distance themselves from the suspected multiple killer was the best defense strategy they could hope for.

At the Crossgates Veterinary Clinic, where Wes Brownell had worked as a kennel assistant, Dr. Jim Anderson said the teen's job would remain open until his case was heard.

The same day as Brownell's release, Woodham's neighbor Merrell Jolly told investigators he had seen Grant Boyette beat Woodham's dog, Sparkle, the previous April while Woodham held the animal down. He said that he'd seen Grant Boyette visit Woodham's house on virtually a daily basis right up until the day before the high school shootings. Jolly also confirmed that he'd seen Donnie Brooks regularly visit the Woodham house until the previous May.

On November 14, 1997, just over five weeks after the Pearl High shootings, local student Chad Allen Parker had a furious argument with a couple of other teens on the Pearl campus of Hinds Community College, just near the high school.

Parker, age seventeen, got in his utility vehicle, drove home, collected a gun, and returned to the school to show those students who was boss. Then he marched into the commons area, just like Luke Woodham had, and headed toward four students standing in a corner area.

To many of the other teens who noticed Parker, with the gun poorly hidden under his jacket, it was like a nightmare reconstruction of the awful event that was still fresh in everyone's minds. But no one dared challenge the teen, who brazenly flashed his weapon at the four students. They saw that his gun was tucked in his belt.

Parker then marched out to the parking lot and got in his car. Police were on the scene within minutes. Parker was apprehended on U.S. 80 and Barnett Drive shortly after he'd left the college. He was charged with possession of a firearm on school property.

Twenty-four

In early November 1997, Woodham's lawyers encouraged Jay Schandler, a correspondent from ABC's *PrimeTime Live*, to visit their client using his other "profession" as a qualified lawyer as a cover to gain entry to the Rankin County Jail.

After a meeting between Woodham and Schandler inside the jail, the program provided lawyers Eric Tiebauer and Leslie Roussell with a video camera. The two attorneys smuggled it into the jail and filmed Woodham while he spoke on the telephone to Schandler.

The two lawyers had insisted Schandler could only put certain questions to Woodham and were equally careful their client answered only what they considered to be points that would be of advantage to him when his case reached the courts.

Behind the scenes, Woodham's lawyers had set up the entire interview because they believed it would show a different side to their client from the angry murderer being portrayed by DA John Kitchens.

The interview aired on November 15, 1997. In it, Woodham talked about his love-hate relationship with Grant Boyette and claimed that his life fell apart when Christina Menefee rejected him.

Luke Woodham once again looked relaxed. But this

time he seemed more wised to the ways of the world and some of the questions brought a positively mischievous look to his face.

"My whole life . . . I just felt outcasted, alone. Finally I found some people who wanted to be my friends," said Woodham. "Everything I did was influenced by Grant. . . . I tried so hard to get his acceptance, you know, 'cause he was the only one who accepted me and the whole time, you know . . . and he just put a lot of bad things into my head and it built up after time, the pressure of everything on top of that I just couldn't take it anymore. I just couldn't take it anymore."

Luke Woodham told ABC correspondent Shandler his life started going wrong from the age of seven when his father left him, his mom, and brother. He talked about how other kids would rib him for reading Shakespeare, Hegel, and Nietzsche. How they didn't like him because he didn't fit in. He refused to name the bullies, but he admitted they made him really mad and filled with hurt.

Woodham said he felt as if he had no friends. Nobody he could trust. As a result he bottled up a lot of problems and started not to care about anything. He claimed he'd wanted to kill himself, but something inside him made him keep going.

Then he met Christy Menefee. But when that finished, he said, there was no one to turn to. He felt totally alone again and then he was introduced to Grant Boyette.

Woodham said Boyette accepted him for what he was. He considered them both special and they became like brothers. Woodham told Shandler that he and Boyette had talked about casting Satanic spells on people. He referred to them as spells that provided power over the devil and things to worship the devil with.

Woodham said everything he did was influenced by Boyette. He admitted Boyette had put a lot of bad things into his head. In the end he couldn't take it.

Most significantly, Woodham insisted that Boyette had wanted him to go to school that day of the shooting. But he claimed he could not remember carrying a rifle onto the campus.

When Woodham said he felt misunderstood, Shandler suggested it was the same for Charles Manson. Woodham retorted angrily that he was talking about Luke Woodham being misunderstood and he insisted he wasn't evil.

When Shandler returned to the subject of Woodham's mother, Mary Anne, Woodham said she was always out partying. Shandler then suggested that Mary Anne Woodham accompanied him on dates with girls. Woodham got angry and refused to talk about it.

Woodham did admit he wished he'd stayed in bed that fateful morning and that he'd had nothing to do with Grant Boyette in the first place. He said he'd like to slap Boyette in the face.

Woodham said he was sorry about Christina Menefee and that he knew how much pain her father was going through.

Shandler's last question was whether Woodham believed he deserved to die. Luke simply answered: "No."

Woodham's interview with the television program seemed to back investigators' findings that suggested the Woodham house became the site where the group of teens plotted the conspiracy to murder Pearl High students.

In the interview, Woodham apologized to the Menefee and Dew families and said he missed his mother and he knew that she would have forgiven him.

One of the most significant parts of the interview came when reporter Shandler asked Woodham if Mary Anne's death was tied to a history of sexual abuse between mother and son.

"You have a sick mind," snapped Woodham, during the phone interview. "Shut your mouth. Shut your lips. How dare you say something like that about my mother?"

Woodham told *PrimeTime Live* that his parents' divorce was the moment that marked his life. Shandler explained, "After the divorce, his mother, he says, began to go out and party a lot, leaving him alone, which further exaggerated his feelings of being alone and that is a time when the guys would come over and hang out at his house."

Legal experts were puzzled by the decision made by Woodham's attorneys to allow their client to appear on a national news magazine program.

At Rankin County Sheriff's Department, an investigation was launched to check the logs of Woodham's visitors to the county jail. As a matter of policy, only attorneys, clergy members, and family were allowed to visit prisoners.

Sheriff Ken Dickerson publicly accused Woodham's lawyers of taking a camera into the jailhouse and then calling the television program on a cell phone.

PrimeTime Live correspondent Jay Shandler admitted he'd met Woodham in the jail for about fifteen min-

utes, a month before the program was aired. He refused to say how he got into the jail.

Woodham's attorneys Leslie Roussell and Eric Tiebauer tried to ease away from the controversy surrounding the program, but eventually confirmed they
had arranged for their client to be interviewed by ABC
on *PrimeTime Live*.

They insisted they were not "media hungry," but
only trying to rebut statements from the prosecution.
Roussell explained, "We addressed the issue with Luke
very early. We told him the media is in this thing, but
we're not in it for the media. We're here to help you.

"He made it clear that he understood that and that
he wanted us to represent him. The only purpose for
ever doing the interview was basically to combat the
thing the district attorney had put out in the media
and try to get a fair shake."

But the plan looked set to backfire since DA Kitchens assured reporters he intended to use a copy of the
taped interview to show that the accused killer was in
full control of his mental and reasoning capacities. He
felt it was quite evident from watching the tape.

Pearl Mayor Jimmy Foster, his family, and many others were deeply disturbed by what they heard on
PrimeTime Live. "I could sense hatred in that voice,"
said Foster. "I don't think there was any remorse there.
Nothing Woodham said shocked me. What shocks me
is that his defense attorneys would let him do something like this."

Pearl Police Chief Bill Slade gained a similar impression: "From what I've seen, he said he's regretful for
what he did, but in the tone of his voice he seems very
cold and callous to me."

What upset many observers in Pearl was the light-

hearted nature of Woodham's reply to one particular
question. "How would everything go if you could turn
back time?" asked correspondent Shandler. "I would
have stayed in bed," answered Woodham with a
chuckle.

Lawyer Eric Tiebauer admitted Woodham had been
fishing around for a new counsel following the storm
of controversy over the *PrimeTime Live* interview. Tiebauer even admitted that he'd told Woodham to call
Jackson lawyer John Colette to "see what he had to
say." Colette said he asked Woodham why he wanted
to hire another attorney.

"You don't understand, those lawyers called me and
they're doing it just for the media coverage," Woodham said.

Colette responded, "I don't think I could work on
those terms."

Woodham's other attorney, Leslie Roussell, insisted
they were not representing Woodham for the publicity
surrounding the high-profile case. They said they were
genuinely concerned with their client's interests.

Tiebauer reiterated claims that the interview en-
abled them to "neutralize" statements made by Rankin
County DA John Kitchens.

Attorney John Colette said he was "appalled" by the
interview Woodham gave to *PrimeTime*. "The problem
with what they've done here is that they've come aw-
fully close, if not crossed the line of hurting their client, by allowing him to make statements on TV," said
Colette. "Those statements will be used against him."

Many observers believed that Woodham's on-screen
apology showed an understanding of right and wrong
that would make it difficult for the defense to present
an effective insanity defense.

To this Eric Tiebauer said, "We feel pretty confident we will get some calls from some psychiatrists. We'll probably meet with a few more of them and make a decision and put a defense together."

In Pearl, the interview was generally perceived as a cheap way for Woodham to get his fifteen minutes of fame on a national platform. The community believed Woodham was looking for sympathy and a little understanding, but they felt little compassion for someone who'd so cruelly put those two young girls into an early grave.

Three days after the *PrimeTime* appearance, Woodham and his lawyers found out for sure why they would live to regret the controversial decision when one of Woodham's classmates filed a twenty-million-dollar lawsuit against the teen.

A lawyer for injured Alan Westbrook explained that the purpose in bringing the lawsuit was to prevent Woodham ever financially benefiting from his crimes.

The suit, filed in Rankin County Circuit Court, requested a jury trial and asked for five million dollars in actual damages and fifteen million in punitive damages.

Amid all the anguish, grief, and sorrow surrounding the Pearl shootings, still very little had been heard or seen of Luke's estranged father, John P. Woodham. It was as if he was determined to keep a distance from his son's actions.

"John's not a bad person. He's actually real gentle on the surface and I'm sure he does care about Luke," said one former work colleague, Susan Mills. "I just think he couldn't handle what happened. He just didn't know how to express his feelings about Luke and this whole tragedy," added Mills, who'd kept in touch with John Woodham for many years.

But toward the end of November 1997, Luke's father made his only visit to see his son in the Rankin County Jail. It was, according to eyewitnesses, a distressing event for both father and son.

"They didn't even say hello to one another. No hugs. Nothing. They hardly said a word to one another. It was tragic and Luke's father only stayed a couple of minutes and then went," said one witness.

The absence of John Woodham was seen as a contributory factor to his son's mental and emotional problems. It was as if John P. Woodham II did not want to stand up and be counted.

Around the same time, Luke Woodham's brother, John, asked investigators for permission to enter his old family home to pick up some items of clothing.

According to Rankin County Sheriff's Department personnel, he also gave his kid brother a wide berth and was only known to have visited him once or twice since his arrest.

Twenty-five

"If you talk you die."

Near the end of November 1997, Kroth member Lucas Thompson received a number of phone calls at his home in which an anonymous caller threatened him with death if he gave evidence against any of the other teens accused of conspiracy in the Pearl High shootings.

Thompson was terrified by the calls. The police tried not to take them too seriously, but DA John Kitchens knew it was vital to get the cases to court quickly before any of his star witnesses began to change their minds.

Lucas Thompson was a virtual prisoner in his own home—too scared to venture out in case he was goaded by his former schoolmates or threatened by those associated with some of his closest friends.

Others involved in the alleged Pearl High conspiracy were apparently not averse to seeking television coverage of their own predicaments. An audio-taped conversation of Delbert "Alan" Shaw turned up on the *NBC Nightly News*. CBS and ABC also played portions of the tape later the same evening.

Shaw had been released the previous week on a

$3,000 bond on the condition he did not talk to the media. Assistant DA Jim Kelly heard the tape, but wasn't sure if it was Shaw. Prosecutors were looking into the matter, but refused to comment any further.

On November 22, 1997—just seven weeks after the high school shootings—it emerged publicly that Grant Boyette had run a *Star Wars* role-playing game that included all the other accused conspirators. John Kitchens insisted that evidence linking the other teens was not solely based on role-playing games.

Kitchens said, "It's not against the law to be part of a role-playing game. There were many other kids who were part of the game who are not subject to this litigation."

One teen, who had played in Boyette's group, was interviewed by investigators and asked detailed questions about the role-playing game. He said afterward, "They [the investigators] were trying to find out as much about the game as they could. I heard the defense is going to play up the fact that they were just playing a game and that Luke simply took it too seriously."

Some legal experts warned prosecutors that if the conspiracy charges were based on the role-playing game, they might run into problems proving the accused teens had a real intent to carry out the conspiracy.

"There would be an argument they could make that the notes they've taken have nothing to do with killing anyone," said retired University of Mississippi law professor Aaron Condon. "The only problem would be convincing the jury that the existence of such notes don't have anything to do with the massacre at Pearl."

* * *

Justin Sledge, facing accessory to murder charges in the Pearl High shootings, walked out of jail on a $50,000 bond on November 25—nearly two months after being arrested by investigators.

Escorted by his attorney, Merrida Coxwell, Sledge made no comment to the horde of waiting newsmen as he left Rankin County Jail at just after 10:45 A.M. Sledge still faced two counts of accessory to murder.

Sledge's bail was the result of delicate negotiations with the prosecution team led by DA John Kitchens. The teen's attorney Coxwell and co-counsel, Dale Danks, Jr., explained, "The fact that bail has been set establishes that Justin Sledge is not a flight risk or danger to the community. This has obviously been a very difficult time for Justin, his family, and all the other lives that have been affected by this matter. Justin and his family wish to express sincere thanks to the hundreds of friends, neighbors, and church members who have provided support during this difficult time."

Even DA Kitchens admitted, "The situation that existed has been completely diffused. If we thought he was a danger to the community, we wouldn't have agreed to a bond."

The bail order signed by Circuit Court Judge Richard Goza imposed a number of stringent conditions:

- Sledge had to report to the county probation office once a week.
- Sledge could not attend Pearl High or enter the school grounds until the charges were resolved.
- Sledge should have no contact with any of the codefendants or witnesses.

- Sledge must have parental or adult supervision while outside his home.

It was also revealed publicly for the first time that Sledge suffered from lupus—an illness that encompasses various diseases from skin lesions to a chronic inflammation that can involve the joints, kidneys, nervous system, and skin. Sledge's form of the illness compromised his immune system and resulted in the teen having to take regular medication.

On December 1, 1997, Luke Woodham underwent more extensive evaluation to establish his state of mind at the time of the Pearl shootings. To prove legal insanity, defense attorneys had to show that Woodham didn't understand right from wrong.

In a court order, Judge Goza agreed to move Woodham from the Rankin County Jail to the state hospital at Whitfield for the evaluation.

Local law experts predicted an uphill struggle for Woodham's defenders because proving insanity in a Mississippi court was one of the most difficult tasks in the nation.

Woodham was to stay the entire month of December in the state hospital and undergo psychiatric and psychological evaluation by experts representing the state and from his own defense team.

Woodham's attorney Leslie Roussell was determined to try to show the jury in his upcoming trials that Luke was not a normal, healthy kid. He wanted them to be convinced that there was something very wrong with the teen.

Also on December 1, Woodham's former friend Delbert Alan Shaw was returned to jail. Shaw had been a passenger in a car pulled over for careless driving at two-thirty A.M. He'd been carrying a thirty-two-ounce beer in strict violation of his bail conditions.

Already out on the bond for the more serious Pearl High charges, Shaw was released a few hours later on $500 bond for the misdemeanor offense of possession of alcohol by a minor.

It was clear that Pearl law-enforcement officials were keeping a close eye on those teens suspected of involvement in the biggest tragedy ever experienced by the community.

On December 13, 1997, a couple of professional writ servers were hired to serve legal papers on Luke's father, John P. Woodham II, at his brother's home just outside Newton, Mississippi.

Scarlett Burrell and her husband, Michael, had spent weeks trying to trace Luke Woodham's only surviving parent so they could serve him with a copy of the twenty-million-dollar civil suit filed against Luke Woodham by attorneys for one of his injured victims, David Westbrook.

Earlier attempts to serve the complaint on John Woodham through his then employer, the state auditor's office, had been ignored by the killer's father.

It was only after a subpoena of John P. Woodham's personnel records at the auditor's office that the writ servers came up with an address for Woodham's mother on Belmont Avenue, just outside Newton, Mississippi.

"He was dodging us," server Scarlett Burrell said. She and her husband knocked on the door of the house and John Woodham answered the door, but then ran back into the house. Less than two minutes later, his brother Richard Woodham rolled up in a car and pulled a gun on them.

The Burrells immediately served the writ by throwing it down on the ground of the carport and left abruptly.

Newton County Sheriff Jackie Knight confirmed that the Burrells had made an official complaint, but he pointed out, "This other guy who pulled up [the brother, Richard] didn't know why they were there. There were strange people at his mother's house at eleven something at night."

The two writ servers weren't the first people to experience difficulties contacting Luke Woodham's father. Repeated calls by journalists to the same house were never returned and phone messages to his place of work were dealt with in a similar fashion

"It's as if Luke's father has completely walked away from his responsibilities as a parent. He just doesn't seem to want to get involved," said one reporter at the time.

Following the Pearl tragedy, changes were made at the schools in the hopes that it would not be repeated.

All school administrators in the entire district were issued cellular phones, and two-way intercom systems were installed in all classrooms to give teachers and students direct communication with the principal's office.

A phone line was installed for parents and community members to call in with any information they thought administrators should know.

Each student at Pearl was required to sign a commitment form promising to alert teachers to any information they thought might lead to someone being harmed.

A full-time Pearl police officer was stationed at the high school and extra security was added for all activities and events.

Suggestion boxes were installed in all schools in the district for students to anonymously submit information to administrators.

Students, teachers, and administrators would attend workshops at the beginning of each school year dealing with character, information, and conflict resolution.

In nearby Madison County, school officials introduced an "intruder drill," whereby each school had a specific phrase for an emergency code meaning an evacuation or lock-down should occur in the classroom. Teachers would receive training on what to do.

In general, more private security guards were to be hired, with police liaison officers becoming much more visible at high schools across the state.

Jackson District Superintendent Jayne Sargent said all the precautionary measures were a step in the right direction. "We want to allay fears of everyone involved and we want to have more adults in the buildings so that if kids see anything that isn't right they'll have enough people to talk to. We want everyone to understand that we're sensitive to the possibility of what could happen at any school and we want everything to be as safe as possible."

But as Obra Hackett, president of the Mississippi Parent Teacher Association, pointed out, "A thousand police officers and security guards probably wouldn't have prevented a tragedy. More attention needs to be paid to what kids are saying. There are signals given. Whether we choose to pick up on them is what makes the difference."

Luke Woodham's one-month stay at the state hospital was supposed to evaluate his state of mind in relation to whether he was mentally responsible for his actions on October 1, 1997.

Hospital staff watched Woodham for twenty-four hours a day, seven days a week. They studied his every move and witnessed no overt psychotic behavior. No demons broke into the hospital and terrorized him. They concluded that he was more than able and fit to stand trial for murder. He also happened to have a 115 I.Q., which was high-average range.

Dr. Chris Lott first tried to evaluate Woodham on December 9, but Woodham refused to talk to the doctor until he had consulted his attorneys. This was later granted. Dr. Lott eventually concluded that Woodham was an angry, resentful, argumentative individual involved in regular bouts of defiant or abusive behavior.

"They typically make excessive demands on others and resent even minimal demands placed on them," was how Dr. Lott summed up Woodham. "They are also typically suspicious of the motives of others and generally avoid deep emotional attachments. They blame others for their problems."

Then he added ominously: "And you know, they do act—tend to act out—they can become aggressive."

Lott also found that Luke Woodham felt he was a special human being, "who feels maybe a little bit better, smarter than others, who feels entitled to typically make demands on others and doesn't reciprocate."

Dr. Lott was also permitted to interview group member Lucas Thompson about Woodham. Thompson had felt that Woodham was definitely smarter, even superior, than most others.

"He and Grant," Thompson told the psychiatrist, "were a little bit—I don't want to say better, but a little bit more intellectual than the others."

Dr. Mick Jepson, who was more sympathetic, also examined Woodham at the state hospital. Even he found Luke's claims about hallucinations difficult to fathom. He believed they were more of a delusional nature. "It just didn't hold true," he later said.

Another doctor who examined Luke Woodham concluded that Luke was essentially narcissistic—a person who required someone who could meet their intellectual or, if you will, egotistical needs.

On December 16, 1997, Grant Boyette was released from Rankin County Jail on a $75,000 bond.

Rankin County DA John Kitchens was furious about the decision and on December 30, he filed a motion with the state supreme court saying that the judge had lacked the authority to release Boyette and that he should remain on the original no-bond order from the court.

In mid-January, Boyette was sent back to jail after the Mississippi Supreme Court overturned the Rankin County circuit judge's earlier decision.

One of Boyette's attorneys claimed that holding his client in jail without bond prevented the teen from assisting with his defense. But for the moment it seemed that Boyette was back in custody.

In February 1998, an attorney for one of the other six teens facing murder conspiracy charges demanded that prosecutors hand over copies of test results on the baseball bat taken from Woodham's home.

Eduardo Felchas, a co-attorney for Donnie Brooks, also asked for body specimen tests taken from co-defendants Grant Boyette, Justin Sledge, and Lucas Thompson.

Felchas claimed that Brooks, whose father was a Pearl firefighter and whose stepfather was a Pearl police officer, wouldn't be able to get a fair trial because of the vast amount of publicity attracted by the case.

In an additional motion for dismissal of the charges, Brooks's attorney described indictments against his client as vague and ambiguous, noting that targets of the conspiracy were not identified.

DA John Kitchens knew that he had an uphill battle to make those conspiracy accusations stick to the teens charged in connection with the Pearl shootings. He was well aware that a conspiracy had to amount to more than just the boys sitting down and saying they intended to commit the crime. The intent on the part of those teens, which went into the state of their minds at the time, also had to be proved.

Judy Johnson, a criminal law professor at Mississippi College, explained, "You've got the act, but it has to be the *real* act. That's the problem with this whole thing."

Boyette's old friend Rick Brown had already given testimony that he believed a role-playing game crossed the line from fantasy to reality and led to the shootings.

Johnson stated that if an agreement was made among a group of members in a fantasy game, but one person took it seriously and actually committed the criminal act, the state would have to show that the other conspirators knew the intent had shifted from fantasy to reality.

Another question likely to face jurors would be whether the alleged conspirators tacitly withdrew from the conspiracy. Under Mississippi law, a conspiracy takes place at the moment of the agreement, regardless of whether the outcome is attempted or achieved.

The fact that three of the accused teens had claimed they'd ended their relationship with Woodham long before the Pearl shootings was a definite plus point for their defense.

DA John Kitchens agreed with other lawmen in Rankin County that Luke Woodham should get two trials—one for the murder of his mother and the other for the school shootings.

It was hoped the trials would take place before the end of the summer of 1998—definitely ahead of the conspiracy trials involving the other teens.

The judge whose job it was to officiate at the trials of Luke Woodham was Rankin County Circuit Judge Samac Richardson, a highly respected law official with a reputation for impartiality that was second to none.

Richardson had received his law degree from the Jackson School of Law in 1975. He was one of the youngest judges in the state when appointed to the Rankin County post in January 1993. Richardson had also served the county as an assistant district attorney from 1982 to 1988, as well as being a public defender for six years previous to that.

In early 1998, it was decided that due to the mass of publicity that had surrounded the case since day one it would be impossible for Luke Woodham to get a fair trial in Rankin County. After much consultation between prosecutors and defenders, it was decided that the venue of the first trial should be a couple of hours northeast of Pearl in magnolia-and-oak-shaded Neshoba, the county seat town of Philadelphia, on the eastern edge of a Chocktaw Indian reservation.

Judge Richardson, now fifty, was no stranger to the Neshoba County Courthouse where his father had been county clerk. More than forty years earlier, Richardson, son of former Neshoba Circuit Clerk Burdette Richardson, had even spent time as a child watching his father work inside the courtroom.

The family of Luke Woodham's first high school victim, Christy Menefee, was so distressed by the constant reminders of their daughter on the streets of Pearl that they moved back to Florida in the early summer of 1998.

"Every day I would have to drive past the high school, or places and stores that she loved to go," said Bob Menefee. "It was just too painful."

The Menefees departed Pearl wondering how the city that seemed to hold so much hope and happiness for them had turned into a community that had, indirectly, cost them their daughter's life.

* * *

At four P.M. on Monday, May 11, 1998, Grant Boyette was once again freed from jail after the Mississippi Supreme Court reversed its position on bond for the accused teen. Boyette was released on $75,000 bail to await trial.

DA John Kitchen knew the decision was a mighty blow to his campaign to have a trial heard as quickly as possible after Luke Woodham's two hearings for the murder of his mother and the Pearl High rampage.

A week later, Donnie Brooks's co-attorney James Bell asked the Rankin County Chancery Court to force authorities to turn over information related to the June 11, 1997, statement his client had given authorities before the Woodham killings.

Bell sought in a motion in the court to depose Pearl Police Chief Bill Slade and others of their knowledge of the statement. He argued that the statement showed his client had withdrawn from any possible conspiracy involving the other teens.

DA John Kitchens was aware that Brooks's statement months before the Woodham rampage could swing the whole balance of his case against the teens for conspiracy.

PART III

JUSTICE

"Whoever fights monsters
should see to it that in the process
he does not become a monster.
And when you look long into the abyss,
the abyss also looks into you."

—Frederich Nietzsche

Twenty-six

Tuesday morning, June 3, 1998, Luke Woodham, now seventeen years old, was shackled and taken out of the Neshoba County jailhouse by half a dozen sheriff's deputies. He was placed in a police van with barred windows, and a cavalcade of deputies' cruisers and two motorcycle outriders escorted him to the Neshoba County Courthouse to stand trial for the murder of his mother.

Woodham's trial virtually brought the square around the courthouse to a standstill. Reporters roamed the streets, satellite trucks from national and regional television stations were parked in every alleyway, and local merchants rubbed their hands with glee at the prospect of an increase in business.

Neshoba, near Philadelphia, had never seen anything like it. "It's the biggest trial we've ever had in our little town," said one local storeowner. "We're not equipped to handle it, but we'll do the best we can."

Woodham, dressed in a short-sleeve shirt and tie, gazed at the vacant jury box and appeared nervous on the first day as the jury selection began. Wearing wire-rimmed glasses and his hair cropped short, Woodham fidgeted with his hands and rarely spoke to either of his attorneys.

His left hand now bore scars. One of them was

shaped like a crescent near the knuckles of his third and fourth fingers.

A small notebook rested in his shirt pocket. His attorney Leslie Roussell later explained that Woodham liked to make notes from time to time.

Roussell remained convinced his client was unlikely to get a fair trial because of the nonstop media attention—even though the trial was a long way from Pearl. Roussell knew he would have to use his finest legal skills for any chance of preventing his client from being found guilty of murder.

Luke Woodham behaved as if he were somewhere else. Courtroom staff described him as "unusually calm" considering the severity of the charges he was facing. It was as if nothing was really sinking in. It was virtually impossible to tell what he was feeling or thinking. He'd shrunk back into the shyness that had enveloped him until the day he hooked up with Grant Boyette and his disciples.

But Luke Woodham had his supporters on hand: a nineteen-year-old from Union and two other teens turned up outside the court to show support for the accused killer, who they believed had been victimized by society. The threesome had even printed a card that read: LUKE WOODHAM, I SUPPORT U. STOP THE HATRED & VIOLENCE.

One of them, Tami Phillips, said, "I think he should be rehabilitated and released. I don't think he would be a threat to society after a while."

No one from Luke Woodham's family—not even his father or grandmother—showed up to offer support for the tragic teen. The Woodham family's nonappearance sparked a degree or two of sympathy for the accused killer.

"It showed the family had no love in it. In a way, it shows how he was raised growing up," said one woman who attended every day of the trial. "Nobody cared. If my kid committed murder, I'd be there no matter what. Family is family. I don't condone killing, don't get me wrong. But then I wouldn't leave my child alone."

Rankin County Assistant DA Tim Jones opened proceedings by describing Woodham's alleged crime to the jury: "He thrilled at murder. He knew what he was doing. Don't be misled by some kind of fantasy theory."

District Attorney John Kitchens delivered a brutally frank statement to the same jury. "There's nothing in the world wrong if you feel sorry for Luke Woodham. We can feel sorry for him. But there's no excuse for killing your mother."

One of the psychological experts to give evidence at the trial, Dr. Chris Lott, labeled Woodham as a "malingerer." Lott explained, "It was my opinion that he was fabricating. It's a little bit stronger than exaggerating. I just didn't believe that he actually ever suffered from a delusional belief such that he saw demons or believed that demons were adversely influencing him."

Another psychiatric expert, Dr. Mick Jepson, called on behalf of the defense, insisted that Luke Woodham "was a very psychologically disturbed youngster whose disturbed thinking and distorted reality left him helpless to judge the appropriateness of his own behavior, to appreciate the implications of his conduct, or to conform his conduct to the requirements of the law."

Dr. Jepson explained how he had carried out numerous tests on Woodham and had concluded, "My test data indicated that it was most indicative of a borderline personality disorder. It was my belief that Luke had been able to conceal his thinking and emotional difficulties by his isolation, essentially in retreating into his own head and not getting around situations that generated strong emotions. He was essentially a loner and used that as a way of trying to control his emotional problems."

One of the key pieces of evidence during the first trial was the manifesto Woodham had handed to Justin Sledge just before he began the shooting rampage.

DA John Kitchens examined it with the help of psychiatrist witness Dr. Mick Jepson sentence by sentence and therefore exposing it to full public scrutiny for the first time.

Kitchens: "Now, tell the jury what the first sentence says."

Jepson: "It says, 'I am not insane.' "

Kitchens: "More?"

Jepson: " 'I am angry.' "

Kitchens: "Okay, does that hold any significance for you as a person doing a psychological assessment on someone?"

Jepson: "Only in terms that I'm going to look very carefully at other data to either corroborate that or oppose that."

Kitchens: "Okay. Go ahead and if you don't mind just read some of it."

Jepson: " 'This world shit on me for the final time.' "

Kitchens: "Okay. Go ahead."

Jepson: " 'I am not spoiled or lazy, for murder is not weak and slow-witted, murder is gutsy and daring.' "

Kitchens: "Go ahead."

Jepson: " 'I killed because people like me are mistreated everyday. I do this to show society, "push us and we will push back!" I suffered all my life. . . .' "

Dr. Jepson went all the way through the contents of Woodham's manifesto and then came to the final sentence.

Jepson: " 'Grant, see you in the holding cell.' "

Kitchens: "Which Grant is he referring to, do you suppose?"

Jepson: "I assume that that was Grant Boyette."

Kitchens: "Okay. Let me ask you a question. Doctor, as an expert forensic psychologist, does any of the language in this particular letter indicate to you that Luke Woodham knew the nature and consequence of his actions and deeds that he took that morning against his mother?"

Jepson: "In that writing, I would say yes."

Kitchens: "Do you think that anything in this writing would indicate to you as a psychologist that Luke knew right from wrong that day?"

Jepson: "Based on that letter, yes, I do."

Kitchens: "Which—which part of that letter?" Kitchens paused while Jepson examined the document. "What about, 'Grant, see you in the holding cell'?"

Jepson: "That. I thought there was another place. 'I am malicious.' "

Kitchens: "So from this writing, you would testify here today that it appears that Luke Woodham, in this writing, characterized the nature and consequences of his acts; is that correct?"

Jepson: "In that writing, yes."

Kitchens also hinged a lot of his case against Woodham on the videotaped confession the teen made just a couple of hours after the Pearl High shootings.

Kitchens pointed out that Woodham did not mention any of his so-called demons or outside forces during that taped interview and he clearly suggested Woodham had "created" devil worshipping and Satanism after committing the three killings to help him win an insanity plea.

Prosecutors called Rankin County Investigator Greg Eklund and forensic experts from Reliagene Technologies, in New Orleans, to show DNA samples and other evidence positively linking Woodham to the murder of his mother.

During cross-examination of Luke Woodham, the subject of his *PrimeTime Live* television interview came up when the prosecution wanted to prove an important point.

Tim Jones: "Isn't it true that you were asked: 'Did you ever feel that your mother was overly protective of you?' "

Woodham: "Yes, sir."

Jones: "And your response: 'She was just a mother.' "

Woodham: "Yes, sir."

Jones: "She was just a mother?"

Woodham: "She was just being her—a mother. She was doing what she thought was right."

Jones: "Did you also say that you knew—that you loved your mother and you knew she forgave you for murdering her?"

Woodham: "I said I knew she forgave me. I never said 'murdering her.' "

Jones: "Okay. But you knew she forgave you. She loved you too; isn't that true, Mr. Woodham?"

Woodham: "I did a lot of bad things, sir."

Jones: "And she loved you?"

Woodham: "Yes, I—I believe that."

Jones: "And in your mind, she would have forgiven you for murdering her?"

Woodham: "Sir, I don't know if I murdered her. And so stop trying to get me to incriminate myself."

Later, Woodham was cornered by Jones about whether his mother really did mistreat him as he had claimed and how he never mentioned it in his many journals.

Turning on Jones with eyes flaring Woodham retorted: "You know nothing about me. None of y'all do. Y'all don't know nothing about me.

"Y'all don't know what I went through. You've never been in my shoes. And you sit here and condemn me for something that y'all don't even know that I did. I—it's not right."

A couple of minutes later, Woodham reiterated to the court that Grant Boyette had told him to kill his mother.

Assistant DA Jones immediately hit back: "That it was the only way? That you loved your mother, but you didn't want to kill her, but it was the only way—because you knew killing your mother was wrong. But it was the only way you could get the gun and the car because she would not just say, 'Go ahead and take it, Luke.' Isn't that true, Luke?"

Woodham shook his head, but said nothing.

Jones: "That's not true?"

Woodham: "You make me sick."

Jones: "Huh?"

Woodham: "You make me sick."

Later Jones returned to the *PrimeTime Live* interview.

Jones: "Okay. Did you tell *PrimeTime Live* that if you

had another chance, you just wouldn't have got out of bed that morning?"

Woodham (sobbing): "Sir, I'm sorry. I can't help that I went to school and I did that. I can't help that. I know I wasn't in control of myself when I did it, and I can't help that. I can't change that. And I'm sorry. I'm sorry. I can't change that. But I don't know if I killed my mother."

Woodham spent the following few minutes crying and insisting that he had no recollection of the death of his mother. Eventually a feeling of sympathy for the teen swept across the courtroom.

Luke Woodham started sobbing again. This time his attorney Eric Tiebauer approached his client and whispered in his ear.

Luke nodded: "Okay."

Tiebauer: "So stop crying for me."

Woodham: "I'm trying."

Tiebauer: "Okay."

At that moment, Luke Woodham looked like any child who has just been caught doing something wrong. For the first time in the entire proceedings there was no talk of Satan or outside influences. This was a child crying because he had no one to turn to.

As Rankin County Investigator Greg Eklund later said, "Luke's just a child. Nothing more than a child. I'm not sure he'll ever grow up."

A model skeleton used by a medical expert to demonstrate how Mary Anne Woodham died leaned against a wall in the corner of the dimly lit Neshoba County Courtroom. Three thin rods in the chest area showed the location of the fatal stab wounds. It cast an eerie eye on the entire proceedings.

At one stage, Kroth member Lucas Thompson was allowed to give evidence to a closed court about his friendship with Luke Woodham and Grant Boyette. The contents of what he said have never been disclosed.

On the third day of the trial, a hushed courtroom greeted Grant Boyette, the most notorious witness of all. Boyette, with his attorney Ed Rainer at his side, responded to Woodham lawyer Leslie Roussell's request to state his name by saying, "Marshall Grant Boyette."

Rainer stepped in, saying, "That's the extent I'm going to allow my client to testify."

Further attempts by Roussell to question Boyette prompted the handing over of a written statement of refusal to incriminate himself. After two more questions, Leslie Roussell gave up.

Attorneys for Lucas Thompson also prevented their client from testifying in open trial after his earlier, private evidence.

Lucas Thompson stated his name; then Circuit Judge Samac Richardson allowed him to invoke federal and state statutes against self-incrimination and answer no further questions.

Donnie Brooks's attorney said his client would have also used the Fifth Amendment protection against self-incrimination if he had been made to take the stand.

* * *

On the fourth day of the trial, the lights went out in the Neshoba County Courthouse, casting jurors in an eerie cavern of darkness. Some attributed the power outage to demons summoned to this small town by the defendant and his onetime buddies. Such was the "weirdness" attached to the trial that some really did think that Woodham was some sort of devil's disciple. The reality was a whole lot different.

In his summing up, Rankin County DA John Kitchens said he didn't believe that Woodham's mother had mistreated him and referred back to the *PrimeTime Live* interview and how Woodham had conceded that he thought his mom would have forgiven him for killing her.

"Doesn't sound like a mother, to me, who would tell, by God, you're going to amount to nothing. That mother went out and worked and fed him and took care of him. And he's hateful and he's bloodthirsty. And he killed her, deliberately and intentionally."

Woodham's lawyer Tiebauer tried valiantly to question some of the forensic evidence from inside the house where Mary Anne Woodham died. He even suggested in a roundabout way that someone else had been in the house at the time.

When it was finally time for the jury to go out and consider their verdict on June 5, Luke Woodham made a point of staring straight at each of the ten women and two men.

Within an hour the Neshoba County jury had found Luke Woodham guilty of murdering his mother. When the verdict was read, a woman in the back of the courtroom wrote the word "GUILTY" in bold letters on a piece of paper and hung it in the back window.

Woodham was sentenced to life in prison. He would not be eligible for parole until he was at least sixty-five years old.

The sound of one juror weeping pierced the silence of the courtroom, but no one was shedding any tears for Luke Woodham—or even his mother. Outside on the courthouse steps, cheers, applause, and screams of joy erupted from the crowd.

Pearl Police Chief Bill Slade said immediately after the verdict that it would provide a small sense of closure for the officers investigating Mary Anne Woodham's murder and the tragedy at Pearl High. He knew the bigger trial for the school shootings would dominate proceedings even more than this one when it happened.

As they loaded Luke Woodham into a squad car outside the courthouse, a last batch of trial watchers, reporters, and cameramen began to clear the courthouse and the rain slowed to a drizzle. A woman rushed forward and was caught for a brief interview by one television crew.

She said, "They ought to shoot him dead because he killed his mamma and he admitted to it. He had the devil in him was all it was."

In the brief run-up to his second trial, Luke Woodham claimed he'd had a religious rebirth and even told his attorney he was going to heaven and his fate was "God's will."

Actually, all that had happened was that one of the pastors inside the Rankin County Detention Center had encouraged Woodham to regularly read the scriptures.

As his attorney Leslie Roussell explained, "I think it's good for him. It gives him some kind of hope in a hopeless world. Jail creates a lot of converts. I think Luke firmly believes in his conversion."

On June 8, 1998, Woodham, wearing a short-sleeve shirt, bullet-proof vest, and shackles, was taken out from the Rankin County Detention Center and driven the eighty miles to Hattiesburg to the Forrest County jail in preparation for his second murder trial. The bustling Deep South city of some 45,000 people was spread out along the northwest edge of the DeSoto National Forest, more than halfway between Pearl and the Gulf of Mexico.

Forrest County jailers were under strict orders to monitor his twenty-four hours a day by closed-circuit TV monitor.

That weekend, severe storms tore through Forrest County, causing extensive damage to property and creating a respite for the relentless legal proceedings of Luke Woodham. The clear-up operation that followed was so extensive that jury selection for Luke Woodham's second murder trial—from a pool of 100 county residents—had to be postponed a day.

DA John Kitchens had gotten into the habit of referring to Woodham's two Pearl High School victims as "his kids." The case had become something of a personal crusade for the tough-talking lawman. His knowledge of Christy Menefee and Lydia Dew was so extensive that, in some ways, he knew more about them than their own families.

John Kitchens felt a genuine responsibility toward "his kids" to see that justice was served. In his eyes, Luke Woodham was a cold-blooded killer who deserved to go to jail for the rest of his life and the second trial had to provide the required result—guilty on all counts.

Twenty-seven

On Tuesday, June 9, 1998, Luke Woodham, un-shaven and wearing wire-rimmed glasses with tape around the left hinge, seemed in a daze, unable to focus on his surroundings as he arrived at the Forrest County Courthouse for his second trial. Wearing a red jumpsuit with FORREST COUNTY INMATE emblazoned across his back, he looked terrified as he was bundled through a crowd of waiting journalists.

Asked by one of them if he could ever forgive him-self, Woodham replied, "No."

Woodham's second trial had also attracted a heavy influx of media from around the world and caused a mini-business boom at Shelby's Coffee Cafe across the street from the Forrest County Circuit Court on North Main Street in Hattiesburg.

Inside the courtroom, the jury chosen to preside over the trial was mostly made up of parents of school-age children.

"You are going to be called on to make credibility decisions in this case," DA John Kitchens told the jury before the case commenced. "You have got to do the judging. You have to decide the facts in this case."

The whole world seemed to be looking on.

* * *

Luke Woodham's shoulders were straight as he stood with his hands in his pockets, sizing up the jurors in the austere surroundings of the Forrest County Circuit Court. Yet within minutes of sitting down at the defense table, he seemed to drift into the sort of daydreaming mode that reminded many of his behavior in the classroom. Woodham slumped forward in his chair, hands clasped between his knees. Occasionally his head moved from side to side, but his thousand-yard stare seemed to be looking at nothing.

Prosecutors told the court how Woodham pummeled his mother with an aluminum baseball bat, fracturing her jaw. Then he stabbed her seven times and slashed her eleven times with a hickory-handled butcher knife while holding a pillow over her face.

They then outlined the full horror of what happened at Pearl High School that same morning.

As the first round of damning prosecution testimony accused him of being a killer with a weird character, obsessed by Satan, picked on by other students, and pathetic, Woodham remained completely stoic.

DA John Kitchens compared Woodham to convicted serial killers, including Charles Manson. "[Woodham] is just mean. He's not insane. He's mean. I think what Luke Woodham has done is, he has followed the lead of other mass murderers."

Woodham's defense team, again headed by attorney Leslie Roussell, insisted that their client was not in a fit state of mind on the day of the rampage. Roussell knew he faced an uphill battle to prove his client was incapable of being responsible for his actions. But it was the only chance Luke Woodham had.

In his opening address to the court, Roussell referred to the courtroom packed with high school students and their families. "It's relevant to the people up there because they suffered extreme loss. We can't dispel their pain, but that's not what we're here to do. We're here to decide if Luke Woodham is guilty. We can't say that Luke didn't do it. He committed the crime." Roussell turned to the jury. "There's no doubt about that. It's a question of whether he's responsible for the crime."

Moving testimony from the seven teenagers who had survived Luke Woodham's murderous attack was due to kick off the first full day of the trial.

Woodham's attorneys offered to stipulate to the events of the shootings to prevent the survivors from having to give painful testimony in open court. DA John Kitchens passed on the offer, insisting some of the survivors wanted their stories heard. He knew just how effective much of that testimony would be in the eyes of the jury.

One victim who spoke to the court was Stephanie Wiggins, a sophomore who spent nearly three weeks in the hospital with a hip wound. She described the fateful moment. "I got hit and went straight to the floor. It sounded like bombs or something."

Student after student painted a vivid picture of the October 1 mayhem. Blood, spent rifle shells, bullets flying everywhere, and wounded bodies lying on the floor that day, littered with dropped book bags.

Jennifer Duke, a junior who witnessed the rampage, started crying when prosecutors asked her to look at Woodham and identify him for the court.

Another Pearl High student, Brook Mitchke, said, "He pointed the gun at me and then he pointed the gun at Christy and shot her. I basically shut down. I started crying."

Mitchke also told the court how her best friend, Christy Menefee, had said Woodham had become a pest to her.

The following day, Luke Woodham came face-to-face with the person he claimed encouraged him to carry out the rampage of death and destruction on October 1, 1997.

Grant Boyette was called to the stand by defense attorneys, but as at the previous trial, he invoked his Fifth Amendment right not to incriminate himself.

Woodham, with his fingertips resting on his lips, watched Boyette with an attentive gaze. Boyette never once looked in the direction of Woodham.

Prosecutors next showed jurors Woodham's video-taped confession made just a few hours after being arrested.

Woodham, sitting with his face down at the defense table, sobbed as the court listened to his interview. ". . . I knew once I killed her. I was going to snap. I just wanted to kill her. . . ."

Quick as flicking on the safety of a hunting rifle, Woodham exploded out of the mist, leaped up from his seat and screamed: "It's just not right!"

He was ordered to sit down or be removed from the courtroom.

The tape continued being played and jurors heard how Woodham had waived his right to counsel, talked about problems at home, and his frustration over being rejected by Christy Menefee.

As prosecutors had also pointed out during his

first trial, Woodham made no mention of Grant Boyette, demons, or gave any indications that he was insane.

Woodham continued to sob as the tape played on.

Twenty-eight

On the final day of his trial, Luke Woodham, wearing a short-sleeve shirt and blue tie, testified for twenty minutes against the advice of his counsel and told jurors he wanted to see Grant Boyette convicted for his part in the high school killings.

Woodham said that Boyette planned to murder Donnie Brooks, Sr., by placing a fat-soluble poison on a doorknob inside the Brooks home. He insisted Boyette put a spell on him that led directly to his actions on October 1, 1997—the day he murdered three human beings. He said that after first meeting Boyette, the older teen told him, "I worship Satan, and Satan's chose you to be part of my group." Woodham added, "He [Boyette] said I had the potential to do something great."

Woodham also claimed Donnie Brooks took a lie detector test and insisted the shootings wouldn't have happened if the Pearl Police Department had taken Brooks's earlier statement more seriously.

There was an uncomfortable shift by some members of the prosecution team as he spoke. DA John Kitchens almost immediately objected to Woodham's remark. Judge Richardson ruled in his favor and ordered the jurors to ignore Woodham's comment.

Woodham told jurors that Satanic spells had

changed him from a student who failed his freshman year to an intelligent person who read books on astrophysics. "I felt like I had complete control and power over a lot of things," he said.

Woodham spoke calmly of friends who twice saved him from suicide. He matter-of-factly described the weird death of Rocky Brewer, the acquaintance who was struck by a car after Woodham and others had put a supposed "spell" on his friend Danny.

Woodham even at one stage conceded to the atrocious crimes he had committed. "The reason this happened is not justified. Nothing can justify that." However, Woodham then pointed the finger at Boyette by saying: "I tried to let it go, but he [Boyette] wouldn't let me drop it. I told him I was having doubts about doing this. He said I had to do it. He said I was nothing. He said I was gutless, spineless and if I didn't do it, I was nothing."

When Woodham was closely questioned by the prosecution, he admitted that it was revenge, not Boyette that was the primary reason why he committed the Pearl High shootings. "I knew it was wrong," said Woodham. "I didn't want to do it."

Woodham refused to say if he was insane on the day of the incident and looked across at the jurors. "I'll leave it in their hands. It's up to them."

Prosecution psychiatrist Dr. Reb McMichael, from the Mississippi State Hospital at Whitfield, said Woodham was motivated by hatred, rage, and jealousy.

Once again, Santa Fe, New Mexico, psychologist Mick Jepson testified for the defense, saying that Woodham suffered from a borderline personality disorder, was under Boyette's influence at the time of the killings and was legally insane on that day.

At five P.M. on June 12, 1998, the Forrest County jury retired to consider their verdict. During those deliberations, three of the jurors vacillated about whether Woodham could have been insane at the time of the shootings. Other jurors pointed out the way that Woodham had talked about the rampage in the videotaped confession and said that should have removed any doubt.

Court reporter Betty Reid was on hand to hear the jury debate the issues. "To a normal person, these acts seemed insane, but that did not mean a person was suffering from an abnormality," Reid said. "To me, an insane person has a medical problem that makes them do bad things. He [Woodham] didn't appear to have a medical problem. There is a tremendous difference in evil and insanity, and this young man was full of evil."

One of the jurors, forty-seven-year-old Randy Temple, agreed. "He's crazy, but he's not insane according to the law. He was easily misled, but he had every opportunity to do what he wanted to do. The boy's real cold-blooded."

The jury could not agree on a verdict. The sticking points remained the question of Luke Woodham's sanity—or lack of it—and whether he was under the influence of Grant Boyette and his so-called Satanic cult.

More than four hours after retiring, the jury finally emerged to read their verdict at just after nine-thirty P.M. on June 12, 1998. Luke Woodham was guilty on all counts of the October 1, 1997, rampage.

Woodham, with Bible selections hanging out of his front pocket, stood with his hands in his pockets and nodded in agreement when Judge Richardson told him he'd acted like a coward.

"It's despicable. It's an outrage," said Richardson. He then sentenced Woodham to two consecutive life sentences, and twenty years on each of the seven counts of aggravated assault, all to be served consecutively.

Judge Richardson asked Woodham if he had anything to say before deputies removed him from the courtroom.

"I am very sorry, Lea Ann," Woodham said, looking across at Lydia Dew's sister. "I know you are my friend, and I know I shot your sister."

For the first time in three days of grueling testimony, Lea Ann Dew Brown broke down, her sobs clearly audible from the back of the courtroom.

"I never had anything against Lydia. She was probably the best person in Pearl," Woodham added quietly.

Then he said in virtually a whisper, "If they could give the death penalty in this, I deserve it. I'm guilty. I am sorry for the people I killed and the people I hurt."

Others, like Assistant DA Tom Jones, claimed Woodham's apology was all a show. "Luke's eating this up," he said. "He loves all this."

After hearing the verdict, the mothers of Woodham's two teenage victims hugged with a mixture of relief and sadness, but Kaye Long and Sheila Jeffers left the talking to other family members. After the sentencing, Lydia's mom, Kaye, could only utter the words, "Thank God."

Christina Menefee's stepmother, Annette Lilly, read a prepared statement on the courtroom steps. "He initiated a chain of events that have wreaked havoc across the country," she said of Luke Woodham. "He should be made an example, but the death penalty is only sought when the murder occurs during a perpetration of a felony.

"Well," Lilly continued, close to tears, "he also stole from us. We will never have the chance to hold Christy, to tell her how much we love her, to look forward to the grand and the great-grandchildren she would have given us."

An even more emotion-filled statement written by Lydia Dew's sister, Lea Ann, came next. "Luke, you said you didn't know you were shooting my sister when you were doing it. But you know it now. I really don't know what to say to you. Jesus, boy! I was your friend. And Lydia was the most gentle, loving person in the world. And you shot her.

"I am okay with the fact she is not on the earth because I know where she is—in heaven, and I am going to try to forgive you, but keep in mind I'll never forget. It will always be in the back of my mind that you took my best friend, my sister, away from me.

"Remember she gave you a hug every morning. She loved everyone, including you, and she probably forgave you the moment she felt that bullet you shot at her . . . remember this: We walk with an angel and her name was Lydia Kaye Dew and you killed her."

Woodham's comments had done little to ease the pain of the grieving families, but Lydia Dew's stepfather, Mike Long, said that his testimony did lead him to believe that Woodham now accepted responsibility for his actions, despite his insanity defense.

"He finally had guts enough to tell the truth," said Long.

Shooting victim Alan Westbrook's father, David, hailed Rankin County DA John Kitchens as a heroic figure who deserved all the support he could get. "John Kitchens did a wonderful job, and I'm proud of him," said Westbrook. "I don't want some pansy in the district attorney's office, and he's done what's needed in this case. To anybody who doesn't like it, they can take it or leave it."

Alan Westbrook said, "He's not insane. He [Luke Woodham] said it himself. He knew what he was doing, went through every step, named everybody he shot."

Westbrook summed up Woodham's demeanor in court. "He sits there, his hands in his lap, and it's like 'Huh, whaddya say about me this time?' "

Also outside the Forrest County Courthouse was Pearl Police Chief Bill Slade, facing yet another barrage of criticism about Donnie Brooks's June statement made months before the high school shootings.

Slade ignored references to Woodham's outburst on Brooks and a polygraph test in court and insisted he was limited about what he could say about Brooks's June 11 statement because it dealt with a youth court matter. He seemed to be using the fact that two of the conspiracy defendants were classified as youths as a reason not to discuss the statement and its implications.

"Brooks came to the department, but it's not like they're trying to portray it," added Slade, who also said the department did not have a lie detector machine. "That's a pack of lies. That's hogwash."

Not surprisingly, Grant Boyette's attorney Ed Rainer also poured scorn on the killer's courtroom claims. "What I heard Luke say last was he's going to try and put Grant behind bars as long as he can. He's still trying to kill people. You can't believe a word the boy said."

The city of Pearl saw Luke Woodham's conviction for the school shooting rampage as a stride forward for the community, but there was still a hell of a long way to go before they had complete closure on the matter. . . .

Luke Woodham was sent to the Central Mississippi Correctional Facility in Rankin County after the trial. Authorities warned him that his long-term destination would be within the notorious walls of the state penitentiary at Parchman. Woodham was going to have to grow up fast or pay the consequences for being young meat in a brutal environment.

Within days of the end of the second trial, Woodham's attorneys filed a motion asking the court to acquit their client or at least order a new trial on the basis that the entire jury was tainted. They argued the jury should have been dismissed because every member—except for one—had read about the case before the court hearing.

Attorneys for three of the other defendants facing conspiracy charges were pressing the Rankin County DA for a trial date for their clients—or an acquittal. DA Kitchens knew it was going to be a tough call, but he refused to bow to pressure and vowed to continue the fight to bring those teens to justice.

He felt an obligation to "my kids," as he always referred to the two young victims, to see this thing through.

Whether justice would be served very much remained to be seen. In legal terms, the fact that Donnie Brooks had provided a statement to authorities four months before the Pearl High tragedy was a minefield.

Kitchens knew that if he was going to avoid being destroyed in the ensuing courtroom battle, he had to avoid the issue.

The problem was that it simply would not go away. And the more the defendants' attorneys pressed him, the clearer it became that someone was going to have to give way.

Twenty-nine

On July 22, 1998, just one month after Luke Wood-ham's imprisonment for the Pearl High school shootings, Rankin County Judge Richard Goza dismissed all the conspiracy charges against Donnie Brooks, Wes Brownell, and Delbert Alan Shaw. They were immediately allowed to walk free from the Rankin County Courthouse.

Charges alleging conspiracy to kill Donnie Brooks's father were also dropped against Grant Boyette, Justin Sledge, and convicted killer Luke Woodham

DA John Kitchens issued a statement saying he still believed the teenagers were involved in a conspiracy, but he had re-evaluated the case after hearing evidence in the two Woodham murder trials.

"The dismissal of the indictment has no bearing on the guilt or innocence in this case," he said. "There was complete chaos at the school. There was constant rumor in that school that you got half the group—you didn't get us all. The law-enforcement authorities acted very prudently with the best interest of the children who were left alive at that school."

John Kitchens, the DA renowned for being unflinching in the glare of the public spotlight, had been boxed into a corner. But even after the dismissal of the charges against the teenagers, Kitchens made no apologies for doing what he considered to be right.

"I wouldn't do anything different," he told reporters. "Everyone said we rushed to justice. If we wouldn't have done anything, we would still have been criticized. Handling a conspiracy case is like walking into an open minefield. If you have other cases that you can prosecute without getting into this quagmire of conspiracy law, it's best to do it."

Kitchens elaborated. "What the state has done in a nutshell is move on now that Luke Woodham has been convicted and focus on what we think are the more serious charges of accessory to murder."

Kitchens's decision to drop the cases against the teenagers had also been heavily influenced by a recent jailhouse interview with Luke Woodham. However, the DA refused to disclose the specific details of the authorities' meeting with the convicted killer.

Judge Goza told the court he would grant a motion to try Justin Sledge and Grant Boyette separately. He said he hoped to have both trials complete by October 1, 1998—the first anniversary of the slayings.

Judge Goza agreed to grant a change of venue for both defendants because of the vast publicity still surrounding the case. Goza encouraged defense attorneys for the teenagers no longer facing murder-conspiracy charges to file motions asking the court to expunge their arrest records.

Judge Goza said he was sympathetic to the need to take quick action to quell fears and rumors around the school through arrests in the days following the shooting. "It's easy to sit here and belittle the police and prosecutors, but you have to remember they were responsible for protecting the students of that school," said Goza.

The people who really mattered—the relatives of the victims—had to face up to the fact that all the wild stories and innuendo that had been sweeping Pearl for so long might not have been entirely true.

Victim Lydia Dew's mother, Kaye Long, was among the court spectators that day. She refused to comment to waiting newsmen, but Lydia's sister, Lea Ann, described herself as "happy" over the dismissals.

Others in Pearl were not so impressed with the judge's dismissal decision.

"It didn't surprise us," said Harriet Westbrook, whose son Alan was wounded in the attack. "These guys need to realize their tails have been saved."

The teenagers themselves were defiant and one of them even claimed it should never have gone so far. Softly spoken Wes Brownell, said, "Everybody who knew me knew it was garbage. I think I'll get over it, but I'll never really forget it."

Brownell would also never forget missing his entire senior year, not going to football games, the prom or graduation.

"I never want to go to that school again," said Brownell, who'd been privately taught during the remainder of the school year.

His mother, Linda Brownell, cried when her son walked through the door and told her the charges were dropped. "There were so many prayers. I didn't know how they could go unanswered," she said. "It's been horrific. There's nothing worse than seeing your child go through something like this. We're talking about some deep wounds, not just some small lacerations."

Brownell's attorney Wayne Milner said after the case against his client was dismissed, "He had no inkling of what was going to happen that morning. He talked to police and gave them a description of what happened and there was no followup to it. He'd done what he thought he was supposed to do."

Wes Brownell did concede he had been friends with Woodham at one time, but again insisted they'd stopped being friends in May, near the end of the 1997 school year. He and his mother refused to elaborate on the reasons why.

Lawyer Milner remained puzzled by the arrest and indictment of his client. "No one wanted to talk to Wes before they arrested him and indicted him," he said.

Milner insisted Brownell was indicted because of guilt by association. "That was an easy jump to make, so from there they [the police] accused him of being involved in a conspiracy."

Donnie Brooks was left virtually speechless when the criminal charges that had hung over him for nine months were dropped. Since his arrest shortly after the shootings, Brooks had been robbed of the life he had envisioned for his senior year.

Minutes after the case had been dismissed, Brooks and his father sat alone in a room off the main Rankin County courtroom and tried to explain to the media what it was like being tied to the horror of the Pearl shootings.

"Most of the time I helped Daddy cut yards," Brooks said of his exile from Pearl High and his life as a student. "I'm glad it's over. It was a total change in my life."

Brooks, Sr., said he had never lost faith in his son despite one of those charges accusing Donnie Brooks of conspiring with three other teenagers to kill his father. He insisted he never believed that Donnie had ever seriously intended to harm him.

"It's been hard for him [Donnie]. But it's made him stronger in Christ. Sometimes hard lessons are the best lessons," said Brooks, Sr., quoting a story of suffering from the Bible.

With the help of a couple of teachers, Donnie Brooks did well enough in his studies to earn two scholarships to Hinds Community College. He was already enrolled for the fall semester.

"The friends I have now have seen me through this," added Brooks.

He knew he'd be singled out following the surge of publicity about the Pearl shootings. "That's to be expected. People are going to do it, and there's nothing I can do about it."

The following day, July 23, 1998, a judge ordered authorities to erase Donnie Brooks's arrest records on the basis that he had been the one person who informed the school of Woodham's intentions long before the tragedy occurred.

Brooks's attorney James Bell said after the decision, "It's finally over. It's a relief that justice is finally done. This young man who tried to do the right thing is free of worry or risk. He'll never be free of the stain, but it's up to him now to make the best of the rest of his life."

* * *

At the end of July, defense attorneys argued for the dismissal of the remaining indictments against Grant Boyette and Justin Sledge. They claimed that the dismissal of the charges against the other teenagers meant, "anything that relates to that crime can't be re-litigated in the future."

DA John Kitchens remained determined to see that some justice was done on the part of "my kids," as he still referred to victims Christy Menefee and Lydia Dew.

The fight for the truth about the worst day in Pearl's history would continue.

In August 1998, Luke Woodham was moved to the notorious Mississippi State Prison at Parchman. He joined a number of very young inmates, sparing him from being treated as a novelty "toy."

However, as one former inmate pointed out, it wasn't exactly a picnic at Parchman either. "At Parchman, they join gangs, get raped. Then if and when they get out, they're worse than when they went in."

Woodham was in with the heavyweights.

On October 1, 1998, to mark the first anniversary of the Pearl shootings, teddy bears, flowers, and signed cards were placed beneath the lighted Pearl High sign on Pirate Cove in memory of Luke Woodham's two young victims. This time there were no sinister messages on behalf of The Alliance of the Immortal. But only one year after the shootings, Luke Woodham's surviving victims found the pain hadn't really eased.

Many in the community had to openly acknowledge that the Pearl shootings had provoked a string of chillingly similar tragedies in schools across the country:

DECEMBER 1, 1997. Teenager Michael Carneal opened fire on students in a prayer circle at Heath High School, in West Paducah, Kentucky, killing three. He pleaded guilty, but mentally ill and will have to spend at least twenty-five years in prison.

MARCH 24, 1998. Andrew Golden, eleven, and Mitchell Johnson, thirteen, shot and killed four students and a teacher at Westside Middle School in Jonesboro, Arkansas. Sentenced to a juvenile detention center, they will be released by the time they turn twenty-one.

MAY 20, 1998. Kip Kinkel, fifteen, killed his parents, then opened fire on fellow students at Thurston High in Springfield, Oregon, killing two and injuring twenty-two. Scheduled to be tried as an adult, he will not face the death penalty because of his age at the time of the crimes.

Trying to forget the tragedy seemed impossible because of those other high-profile shootings across the nation. Every time it happened somewhere else, Pearl got a mention as the precursor. There seemed to be no escape from the crimes of Luke Woodham.

On the day of the Pearl High anniversary, Christy Menefee's family took the day off from work and spent time together at their new home in Florida. Her parents' wedding anniversary fell on the same day, but they moved it to the previous day, September 30.

The Menefees had tried hard to pick up the pieces

of their shattered lives, but Christy's father, Bob, admitted, "It's a day-to-day thing. A lot of times you feel your strength failing and your whole world feels like it's ending. But you have to move forward."

Bob Menefee and the rest of the family had seen certain things during the previous year that at least helped to ease some of the wounds, including the Woodham conviction and the passing of a law to expand the death penalty to include people convicted of campus killings. Bob Menefee had also made a number of talk-show appearances, as well as giving lectures to families of other school shooting victims. He planned to write a book about his daughter's life.

But he could never see the day when the family would completely recover. "We have to go on with our lives. We have to go to work and live," he said. "You can't just stop. But although we're doing okay, it will never go away. Time dulls the pain, but it will always be there."

Some of the surviving teenagers from Luke Woodham's rampage were also suffering one year on from the atrocity.

Deepika Dhawan, now eighteen, had been shot in the left shoulder. She'd only been in the country for a year after arriving from India. The teenager had such a hard time dealing with the aftermath of the shooting that she and her family moved to Vicksburg just weeks later.

For junior Jerry Safely, the memories of being shot still lingered. "October 1 is just another day," he said. "I've tried to put it behind me and stay involved in things with school."

Pearl Mayor Jimmy Foster, whose son Kyle was one of Woodham's alleged targets, said his son had completely blotted out the tragedy. "Everybody's ready to get it behind us and I think we have," Foster said. "Kyle doesn't ever say anything about it. He's too busy on other things."

Foster admitted that in the city of Pearl, the blasts from Luke Woodham's hunting rifle had shattered other people's calm forever. Many residents no longer had a sense that their town, strong on family values and rich with youth sports programs, was immune to the sort of violence associated with the big cities like Los Angeles and Detroit.

"Now we understand that these things can happen anywhere," said Jimmy Foster. "I think the hardest thing we had to understand and get over ourselves was the idea that we were one of those places where this couldn't happen."

Many locals in Pearl now braced themselves every time they heard police sirens near the high school.

At the Woodhams' abandoned house on Barrow Street, neighbors noticed that people still drove by to look at it.

The driveway was covered in leaves and the windows were as dirty as ever, so it still retained that look of unkemptness that had always been the house's trademark when Mary Anne Woodham was alive.

On a few occasions, local kids from Pearl High were seen screaming torrents of abuse at the house as they walked by. Some even stood on the porch.

It was as if the property somehow was to blame for the appalling tragedies that happened on that October day.

Thirty

On October 10, 1998, a circuit court judge postponed Justin Sledge's trial date following a joint motion from prosecutors and the defense team. Both sides admitted they still intended using testimony from Luke Woodham in the eventual trial.

Rankin County DA John Kitchens made a decision many believed might deeply affect the cases against the two suspected teens, Boyette and Sledge. Kitchens decided he'd had enough of fighting in the trenches of the war on crime and wanted to be a general—in other words, a judge.

He became one of four candidates vying for two circuit court judicial posts in the 20th district of the state. His rivals included Judge Samac Richardson, the man who had presided over the two Woodham trials.

It was a tough decision for Kitchens since he was fully aware that it would mean he would not be around to fight through all the charges against Grant Boyette on behalf of "my kids."

Kitchens's decision prompted a gloomy feeling throughout the community of Pearl that the remaining trials might never happen. There were genuine fears that any new incoming district attorney might not see the point in pursuing with energy the conspiracy charges still hanging over Justin Sledge and Grant Boyette.

On November 11, 1998, Grant Boyette was arraigned on an accessory to murder charge stemming from the death of Mary Anne Woodham. This came in addition to his accessory to murder charges in connection with the Pearl High shootings.

Prosecutors had testimony and statements from witnesses, including Boyette's old friend Rick Brown, talking about the phone call between Woodham and Boyette in the early hours of the morning of Mary Anne Woodham's murder.

Boyette pleaded innocent to the charge in a preliminary appearance at Rankin County Circuit Court.

This latest indictment came following yet another jailhouse interview conducted with Luke Woodham by members of the Rankin County DA's office.

Deputy DA Rick Mitchell explained: "We honestly felt there was enough evidence for this charge and the grand jury felt there was enough evidence to indict him."

Grant Boyette's lawyers, Ed Rainer and John Emfinger, presented no witnesses during the Rankin County Circuit Court hearing. "Whether or not we brought fifteen people in to offer their opinions, it still would have been the judge's decision," explained Emfinger.

No new trial date was set.

On that same day, it was also disclosed that Boyette's other trial on the previous charges connected to the school shootings had been postponed until a new location could be found. The judge had agreed to move it because of the publicity surrounding the case.

Boyette rushed from the side door of the courthouse, refusing to comment to waiting reporters while his attorney Ed Rainer admitted his client was "stoic, upset and disappointed" about the fresh charges.

On December 21, 1998, a Rankin County circuit judge ruled that Justin Sledge wouldn't have to stand trial on charges of accessory before murder after all. Judge Goza withdrew the indictment against eighteen-year-old Sledge after a grand jury said there was not enough evidence against him.

Sledge's attorney Merrida Coxwell said afterward evidence that influenced the grand jury included a taped interview with Luke Woodham in which he exonerated Sledge from involvement in the events of October 1, 1997.

Coxwell also insisted his client had no hard feelings toward Pearl police investigators and other authorities who had earlier arrested and charged him.

"I think the law-enforcement officers were well intended, but probably jumped the gun with some of their arrests," explained Coxwell. "He now wants to move ahead with his education." Sledge had endured a total of fifty days in jail and the loss of his junior year at Pearl High because of the charges hanging over him.

Shortly after his release from the charges, Sledge issued a statement through his attorney in which he said, "The isolation, fear, and utter hatred directed toward me were the things I remember most. Friends and school peers turned their backs on me and I realized that a conviction in the eyes of my friends was a prison in itself."

Sledge planned to finish the eleventh grade and high school and he revealed that he'd been volunteering for a Jackson community service organization over the previous few months.

Sledge believed he was made one of the scapegoats for the mood of hysteria that swept Pearl in the days following the shootings. "Reflecting upon the horrid days following the Pearl High shootings, I can now see the turmoil that the city of Pearl was thrust into and the high emotions that caused the resulting arrests."

Sledge insisted he still wished the community well. "I hope that the city of Pearl and all my friends and fellow students can move beyond the tragedy. My heartfelt condolences go out to all those who were injured or lost loved ones that day. My true friends, my church, and my legal counsel each had an unwavering belief and faith in my innocence. To you I offer thanks from the bottom of my heart."

Pearl High shooting victim Jerry Safely doubted Sledge would re-enroll at his old school and warned that although the charges had been dropped, many people would "not forget it."

The trial of Grant Boyette, charged with accessory to murder before the fact, was imminent. Or so it was presumed until mid-December 1998, when a court in Warren County postponed the hearing because of construction work in the Vicksburg courthouse where the trial was due to be heard.

Grant Boyette's defense team knew only too well that the longer the gap between trials the better. And the case against him was in no way cut and dried.

There was a feeling in the community of Pearl that

until the matter was brought to a conclusion, they would remain haunted by the events of October 1, 1997.

In late December 1998, a civil lawsuit was filed in Rankin County Circuit Court on behalf of Kaye Long, the mother of Pearl High victim Lydia Dew, charging the parents of all six of the teenagers connected with Woodham of negligence. The suit also named the Pearl Public School District as a defendant.

The suit accused the teenagers of being members of the Kroth, which prosecutors had already characterized during Woodham's trial as being a cultlike group.

It also stated that the teenagers' parents "knew or should have known their children were members of a Satanic cult." Failure to do so, the suit claimed, constituted negligence.

Jerry McKernin, of Baton Rouge, an attorney for the Menefee family, announced that the Menefees would also soon be filing the lawsuit they first talked about a few months after the tragedy.

In January 1999, Grant Boyette was told he'd be unlikely to face a trail for several more months. No venue had yet been agreed upon by the judge in the case. Boyette and his defense team were delighted.

They remained convinced that time would heal some of the awful psychological wounds inflicted by Luke Woodham's rampage of death and destruction at Pearl High School. That could mean a respite for their client and what they claimed were the wild accusations linking Boyette to the events of October 1, 1997.

In February 1999, it was announced that the same judge who had presided over both the Woodham trials would be in charge of the Grant Boyette hearing. Once again Circuit Judge Samac Richardson was forced to defend himself. He insisted he would not be stepping down, despite defense attorneys' suggestion that his earlier role could lead a "reasonable person" to doubt his impartiality.

Richardson insisted, "This is a different case, a different defense, and different lawyers. It could be the same evidence, same witnesses. But because I made rulings in one trial does not mean I'll make the same rulings in this case."

Richardson publicly stated that he hoped the Boyette trial would go ahead no later than July 1999.

As fear and trepidation about school killings swept the nation in the early months of 1999, Rankin County Investigator Greg Eklund found himself being consulted by law-enforcement officials from across the nation because of his Pearl High experiences.

He even took part in a seminar in Little Rock, Arkansas, hosted by the FBI at which lawmen and teachers from schools in Jonesboro, Arkansas, and Springfield, Oregon, were present.

"When those other shootings happened, the first thing we did was call them up and say, 'Look, your people can work the scene, work the crime, but what you have to be ready for is the onslaught of the media, because it is going to be unbelievable,'" explained Greg Eklund.

The Little Rock seminar was not open to the press because it was felt that the less publicity created by it, the better as that might simply encourage teenagers to take the law into their own hands. However, the entire seminar was taped and later turned into a CD entitled "Lessons Learned."

A few weeks after the seminar, it became painfully obvious that little had been learned from these tragedies. Memories of Pearl came flooding back into the community when the Columbine tragedy exploded on April 20, 1999.

Students Eric Harris and Dylan Klebold opened fire and tossed grenades as they stormed the halls of Columbine High School in Littleton, Colorado, killing twelve students and one teacher before taking their own lives.

The latest, most brutal school attack of all reminded Mississippi residents to be on their guard against any more such incidents.

Rankin County investigator Greg Eklund—who probably did more than any other officer in regard to the Pearl High case—spoke to police in Jefferson County, Colorado, and was able to offer them valuable follow-up advice.

Just a couple of days after Columbine stunned the world, police were called to Clinton High School, near Pearl, to question a student about a threatening drawing.

A few days after that, two Mississippi teenagers were arrested after drawing threatening pictures of people in trench coats.

In nearby Forrest County, an eleventh grader was arrested and thrown in jail after allegedly calling in a bomb threat. His case was due to go before a grand jury.

A sixteen-year-old was accused of aggravated assault after an incident at his school in Pike County, Mississippi.

At the Southern Baptist Educational Center in Southaven, a fifteen-year-old pulled a gun from his backpack, placed a bullet in the chamber, and threatened to kill himself.

The negative reaction against students wearing trench coats was so strong after the events in Columbine that students who wore such a "uniform" were threatened with suspension from class if they wore the clothes to school. Two seniors at Tupelo High, Mississippi, were given three days of in-school suspension for wearing trench coats to campus.

Following Columbine, Mississippi area school districts, including Pearl, met to discuss ways of making their facilities safer. Deputy Superintendent Ron Sellars briefed principals about a guide that was being distributed to schools across the nation by the U.S. departments of Education and Justice.

"We wanted to raise their awareness and to give them sources they can use for schoolwide safety plans," explained Sellars.

Some believed it was all a case of too little, too late.

At the end of May 1999, Pearl High Assistant Principal Joel Myrick left the high school campus for the last time. He was moving to a new job as principal of

Corinth High School, located in the north of Mississippi.

Pearl Mayor Jimmy Foster reflected the feelings of the entire community when he said, "He [Myrick] put his life on the line with no regard for himself to save as many kids as he could. He will always be remembered for that."

Not long afterward, Myrick received the Valley Forge Cross for Heroism Award at the National Guard's conference in Atlanta.

More disturbing in some people's eyes was another award given to Myrick by *Soldier of Fortune* magazine. The former Pearl official insisted he had no qualms about accepting the award as 1999 Humanitarian of the Year, despite the publication's extreme right-wing reputation.

In June 1999, Pearl High School Principal Roy Balentine shared his knowledge of conflict resolution with 300 educators and law-enforcement officials at a "Stop the Violence" conference sponsored by Mississippi's Department of Education Office of Safe and Orderly Schools.

"There is no way you can know what it's like until you have walked in the shoes I have worn," explained Balentine. "I would never have thought this could have happened in Pearl or in Mississippi when I arrived at work that morning."

But, he told the conference, the reality was that there were students who valued recognition over achievement, who were often neglected by parents or adults and at odds with their peers.

Balentine then spoke specifically about Luke Woodham. "I doubt if Woodham was thinking about what would happen when he cut his mother's throat. He is probably thinking how dumb he was, serving three life terms plus 140 years in prison."

Balentine revealed that he had devised his own step-by-step way of dealing with conflict between teacher and student:

- Explore the other person's position
- State your position
- Create a statement of the problem to be resolved together
- Generate alternatives
- Select a solution and agree on an action plan

"I'm not going to stand here and tell you this will prevent all school violence," Balentine said. "But we cannot sit and wonder if it is going to happen again and when it is going to happen and not put these steps into action."

Balentine emphasized that, on balance, schools are safe. "Every two days, eleven children die in domestic violence," he said. "We need to keep school violence in perspective. School is still one of the safest places for a child to be, but we have to keep working to make them safer."

Since the Pearl tragedy, Balentine had spoken at seminars in Georgia, Ohio, Mississippi, Alabama, and Canada, and had appeared on national television, including *The Today Show*.

School shootings had instilled fear and trepidation in families across the nation.

Thirty-one

In all prisons there is an environment in which the folks who do the best in terms of survival are the strongest. They prey on the weak. The weak prey on the weaker.

Luke Woodham found himself firmly at the bottom of that pile in the state penitentiary at Parchman.

He could of course have considered joining a gang, but a typical Parchman initiation made Grant Boyette's Kroth look like a kindergarten.

Just before Woodham arrived at Parchman, gang hopeful Jerry Larry was hit twelve times directly over the heart as part of an initiation "ceremony." His heart failed completely on the twelfth blow.

Gang "zone enforcer" Desmond Durr of the Black Gangster Disciples at Parchman was in charge of administering such "love licks" to prospective members. He was later convicted of the manslaughter of Jerry Larry.

Perhaps it was lucky that geeky, bookish Luke Woodham was not high on the recruitment drive list for the prison gangs at Parchman. But one thing was very clear: Luke Woodham was going to have to grow up fast if he was going to survive in hell.

* * *

In the middle of 1999, Secret Service agents visited Luke Woodham at Parchman. They wanted to conduct a series of taped conversations with him as part of their research into the mentality of killers.

Woodham was fascinated and intrigued in a child-like way by his meeting with the Secret Service and immediately gave permission for the interviews. For reasons known only to himself, he chose not to tell his attorneys, who were still putting together an appeal against his convictions for murder.

In the secretly conducted interviews, Luke Woodham talked about his motivation for the killings and admitted, "I couldn't find a reason not to do it."

Woodham expressed regret and once again blamed his difficult childhood for the feelings that led to the shootings. "It's real hard to live with the things I've done," Woodham told the Secret Service. "I just didn't have anyone to talk to about all the things I was going through."

He added: "I kept a lot of hurt inside me. I just felt like nobody cared."

Woodham told his interviewers about some of the malicious teasing he endured at Pearl High. "They'd always talk about me and push me around and start fights with me and stuff." He said the experience "made me really angry."

Woodham got on extremely well with the two Secret Service agents who visited him at Parchman and has remained in written contact with them to this day.

In prison, Luke Woodham had become a prolific letter writer. Just after the Secret Service interview, he

wrote to one of the investigators most responsible for
his life prison sentences.

Rankin County investigator Greg Eklund said he
wasn't that surprised to get the letter, which he still
keeps as a memento on his desk at the county sheriff's
office.

Eklund explained: "It's not remorseful. Luke has
shown absolutely no remorse for the victims, or about
his mother or even those other kids in his school. Not
one bit of remorse."

Woodham's letter asked Eklund how he was doing
and urged him to write back. Detective Eklund says he
has no intention of doing so.

"Luke is a child. He was a child when he did this
and he is a child basically now, even though he is serving successive life terms at Parchment Penitentiary
with an additional 140 years on top of that." Eklund
continued, "I don't even think Luke fully appreciates
that I am the one who helped put him there."

Greg Eklund is waiting for the day when Luke Woodham actually "comes out and tells us the whole story
of what happened when he killed his mother. But we'll
most probably never know."

Luck, if nothing else, continued to be on Grant
Boyette's side as he awaited his trial in connection with
the killings carried out by Luke Woodham.

The case had been relocated to Biloxi in the summer of 1999, but that long-awaited trial was yet again
postponed in September that year when one of the
case's most crucial witnesses dodged a court subpoena.
The missing witness was onetime alleged coconspirator

Lucas Thompson. Judge Samac Richardson admitted
that the teenager had gone completely AWOL.

Law officials had failed to find any trace of Thompson
in Mississippi and that presented attorneys with a huge
problem. Judge Richardson explained, "The jurisdiction of this court or any state circuit court doesn't go
beyond the state of Mississippi. Subpoenas issued by the
clerk of the court can be served anywhere in Mississippi,
but we have no jurisdiction over any party outside the
state."

Grant Boyette remained free on bond and continued his life relatively untouched by the tragedy many
believed he was responsible for causing.

At the state correctional facility at Parchman, Luke
Woodham continued to find himself surrounded by
murder and mayhem. No wonder he'd turned to the
scriptures.

On death row in notorious Unit 32, self-confessed
serial killer Donald Leroy Evans was stabbed seventeen
times by a fellow death row inmate who'd made himself a shank. Questions were immediately asked as to
how the killing occurred, as all death row inmates were
supposed to be restrained with waist and leg irons at
all times in single cells. A lot of speculation centered
around the prison authorities "turning a blind eye"
to the killing.

Luke Woodham wondered if they'd do the same to
him if he got caught by a homicidal maniac with a
homemade knife.

Most prisoners tended to avoid much contact with
Woodham, as his status inside Unit 32 was not as
clearly defined as that of the majority of inmates. He

wasn't a fully fledged bank robber or sex offender. He also couldn't be defined as a pedophile. He just didn't fit in. It was a lot like being outside in the real world.

For his own part, Woodham tried to keep out of everyone's way by spending as much time as possible reading, and writing letters and poetry.

On November 29, 1999, a date was finally agreed upon for the trial of Grant Boyette, who was still facing three counts of accessory to murder for allegedly masterminding the shooting rampage at Pearl High.

The trial—already twice postponed—was scheduled to take place in Biloxi on February 28, 2000.

Attorney Ed Rainer, who represented the now twenty-one-year-old Boyette, had managed to get the hearing put back because "we were unable to secure through subpoena the attendance of certain essential witnesses." Rainer did not identify those witnesses, but it was presumed that the missing Lucas Thompson was among them.

On February 3, 2000, Grant Boyette was hauled before the Rankin County Court to be re-indicted on the charges he faced in connection with all of Luke Woodham's killings.

Many saw newly installed DA Rick Mitchell's insistence on re-indicting Boyette as a scare tactic designed to let Boyette know that authorities would seek maximum punishment against him when his trial went ahead later that month.

Behind the scenes, Boyette's attorneys and the

prosecutors, led by Mitchell, were trying to bring about the complete closure of the case against Boyette.

Mitchell's attitude was that too many man-hours and vast amounts of money had already been spent on the case to date and it had to be brought to a speedy and satisfactory conclusion.

He even went to the effort of consulting the families of Woodham's two student victims to see how they felt about "striking a deal" with Boyette's attorneys. None of the relatives objected because they had gotten to the point where they just wanted the trials to finish so they could try to rebuild their lives.

Five days later, Grant Boyette pleaded guilty to a lesser charge of conspiring to impede a public official. In exchange, prosecutors dropped the more serious murder-accessory charges that directly tied Boyette to the three slayings committed on October 1, 1997.

In the new charge, prosecutors said Boyette encouraged Woodham from March 1 to October 1, 1997, by discussing acts that would disrupt the school and prevent school officials from doing their job. They referred to testimony from witnesses saying that Boyette often talked about going into the school and used language such as creating chaos in the school and even taking over the school.

DA Rick Mitchell had also taken the difficult decision to go for a deal because he didn't think Luke Woodham—a convicted triple murderer—would prove a credible witness for the prosecution.

In a petition filed in the Rankin County Circuit Court, Boyette maintained his innocence and said he only entered a guilty plea to take advantage of the deal on offer.

DA Mitchell made a point of publicly referring to

how he'd consulted the families and law officers about the intended plea agreement and they had backed the decision. "The fact is there's no evidence that he made a dry run at the school, that he went out and they staked out the school, that he showed him [Woodham] how to use a gun or he furnished weapons or he furnished the vehicle or he furnished the ride to school," said Mitchell.

Boyette's lawyer Ed Rainer was extremely candid about his client's involvement in the tragedy when he admitted Boyette did talk with Woodham about causing trouble at the school. "He [Boyette] was the master of games because of his imagination. Then they began talking about doing bad things, like teenagers do," said Rainer.

Woodham's attorney Leslie Roussell had a rather different take on the case's outcome. "Sounds to me like it was a way to sweep an unpleasant case under the rug and still save a little face in the process."

Three days later, Boyette was sentenced to a five-year sentence, all of it on probation if he completed a boot-camp–style Regimented Inmate Discipline program (RID).

Grant Boyette was later told he would have to spend the first month of his sentence at the Central Mississippi Correctional Facility in Rankin County while he went through a classification process. The RID program that followed would take a minimum of twenty weeks.

It would be tough, but nothing compared with the lifelong regimen of brutality and fear that Luke Woodham was already facing inside a real prison.

* * *

Grant Boyette's light sentence left many Pearl residents bewildered and bitter. "A mastermind like that ought to have to serve fifteen years flat, at least," said Pearl resident Robert Parman, a Vietnam veteran, former Army Ranger, and army drill instructor.

However, Pearl's tough, no-nonsense Mayor Jimmy Foster said he had no problem with the sentencing. "It's finally over. I think it came to the best possible conclusion we could have had," said Foster. "We've got a guilty plea and a permanent criminal record. It's time for us to move on. We can finally close this whole sad chapter."

Meanwhile the American wheels of justice continued to turn in the only way they could. Boyette's guilty plea on the lesser charge had cleared the way for a civil trial connected to the Pearl slayings.

Pearl Public Schools District knew only too well that they had been accused of being negligent in a civil suit filed by Lydia Dew's mom, Kaye Long. Their attorney, Michael Hartung, said his number-one priority was to depose Boyette and possibly Woodham.

But Hartung admitted to reporters: "Frankly, I'm more interested in Boyette. Poor Woodham was one of those sad little creatures that we all know a few of in our lives. He's not very smart. He's easily persuadable."

The civil trial was expected to go ahead in the late summer of 2000.

Another former member of Grant Boyette's Kroth had new problems on the horizon.

On February 16, 2000, a couple of days after Boyette's sentencing, Donnie Brooks was charged at the

Brandon City Court with embezzlement and five counts of false pretense.

Brooks, now twenty-one, was living at a house on Twin Pine Lane, Pearl, that he owned and shared with his girlfriend. Brooks was arrested at his home when police seized more than $6,000 worth of stolen computer equipment after a tip.

The hardware was allegedly taken from a Brandon law office where Brooks had been working as a nine-dollars-an-hour computer network administrator eight weeks earlier.

Police set Brooks's bond at $25,000. If convicted of embezzlement, Brooks could face a maximum ten years in jail and a $10,000 fine or a $1,000 fine and one year in jail.

Thanks to Brooks's alleged connection to the Pearl High shootings, his arrest made front-page news in the local press.

Excerpts from Luke Woodham's supposedly secret taped interviews with the Secret Service turned up on a *60 Minutes II* episode about research into the mentality of assassins in March 2000. The agency claimed they were trying to create a profile that could then be used to recognize a would-be killer and help prevent attacks.

Woodham's lawyer Leslie Roussell immediately claimed that his client's rights may have been trampled by the public release of the videotape. "We didn't know anything about this interview. Frankly, I only read about it in today's Jackson newspaper," Roussell told reporters.

He was concerned that the public release of the tape

came at a time when he still had an appeal pending before the Mississippi Supreme Court. Roussell and fellow defense counsel Eric Tiebauer had asked the network not to air the program, but they ignored the lawyers' request.

60 Minutes II defended use of the videotape because the interview had been conducted by federal agents, not the news magazine show itself.

In fact, the program only featured about thirty-five seconds of the Woodham interview and the Secret Service had obtained a release from Woodham himself, as well as from officials of the Mississippi's Corrections Department, before the excerpt was screened.

Roussell remained angry. "I think it's pretty shady to go around a minor's attorney to get some sort of authorization to air it when, from our point of view, Woodham was not competent to make that kind of decision."

Roussell genuinely believed that if the state supreme court reversed the jury's earlier verdict on Woodham and granted a new trial, then everything said by Woodham in the interview could be used against him later.

"You don't know if you can get a fair trial anyway, and this would certainly make it harder," added Roussell. "When the first trial occurred in Mississippi, he was enemy number one anyway, and now we have this."

On the same television program, Secret Service psychologist Robert Fein said that the behavior of teenage school shooters was similar to people who had made attempts on the lives of public officials.

"They are not deliberate actions where people suddenly snap," explained Fein. "They occur after days, weeks, months of deliberation."

* * *

On a slab of concrete behind a fence rimmed with razor-sharp barbed wire, a regiment of about fifty men marched in solid straight lines. Wearing identical powder blue hats and military-style fatigues, they were ordered to keep their hands tightly curled around the seams of their pants. Faces void of expression, the rhythmic thud as they marched made it sound like an army camp.

Among them was Grant Boyette in the early weeks of the Regimented Inmate Discipline program. Boyette's sentence to boot camp was not the easy option some people had felt it was. Boyette found himself among a group of men ranging in age from thirteen to thirty-nine. He knew he was extremely fortunate because, as a first-time offender, he'd been assigned to the RID program. The idea behind the RID was to expose offenders to such a rigorous program that they'd never be tempted to re-offend—and it was supposed to help curb prison overcrowding.

By a strange twist of fate, Grant Boyette found himself in a RID unit at Parchman, where his old friend Luke Woodham was also incarcerated. Luckily for Boyette, the program kept all its offenders separate from the general prison population. Boyette was expected to buckle down and obey every order.

As RID Commander Joe Erringham, explained, "RID gives them a sense of accomplishment. If they successfully complete the program, as hard as it is, they can be proud of themselves. They know they can do anything."

In Grant Boyette's case, he already believed he could

do everything and that was where his problems had begun.

Just a few hundred yards away, Luke Woodham was learning how to live life on a unit inhabited by murderers, serial killers, rapists, and child molesters.

Unit 32 at the state penitentiary in Parchman is chillingly referred to as "a prison within a prison." It is used to house inmates in protective custody, a category that includes those considered in peril, as well as those themselves who are a danger.

Woodham found himself in the most security-conscious part of the prison. He and all other inmates were searched every time they left their cells. They could only move outside their cells if they were in leg and waist irons to limit their movements.

When twenty-seven-year-old inmate Shannon David Truelove was stabbed to death by another Unit 32 inmate, it once again did little to reassure Luke Woodham that he was safe from attack.

"Despite the best interests of the penitentiary, if an inmate makes up their minds to kill someone, they're going to get to do it sooner or later," former Parchman Superintendent Don Cabana pointed out.

Shannon Truelove had been stabbed once in the back of the neck, twice in the right arm, and five times in the right side and chest. Guards took more than five minutes to get to the scene as no one bothered to raise the alarm.

Mississippi had long been considered the "lockup" capital of the entire country. Population-wise, Mississippi kept more people behind bars in state and county jails than anywhere else. The biggest irony in the case of Luke Woodham was that it cost four times more per day to incarcerate him than to educate him at Pearl High School.

At least five inmates were stabbed to death during the first eighteen months Luke Woodham spent inside Parchman. The killings were no surprise to the more hardened inmates who knew that anything from a metal strip off a postal package to sharpened pieces of plastic piping could be turned into lethal weapons.

However, prisoners' ingenuity could be turned to more use sometimes. On one occasion, prison staff had to close down a machine that wasn't working properly only to discover hot baked potatoes stuck inside the exhaust pipe.

Rankin County Investigator Greg Eklund had a closer involvement with the crimes of Luke Woodham than most and he remained—even after the Grant Boyette "deal"—convinced that more Pearl–style tragedies would happen.

"When you deal with something like this, everyone can sit back and be an armchair critic and say there were obvious signs," said Eklund. "Hindsight is always twenty-twenty, but if you have to make a split-second decision on what you should do, who's in charge of what, it can be very taxing. You cannot ever dictate where these things will take place."

But Eklund harbored real fears that school killings across the nation would get more serious, more sophisticated. "Each one seems to have a little bit more pre-planning and that is very worrying," said Eklund. "That's the frightening thing. I don't wish to be derogatory about the media, but I feel that it has played a big part in this because these kids are seeing what's happened and are saying they want to do better."

Eklund was struck by the similarities between the events in Pearl and Columbine—the trench coats, the war plan to destroy the school, the escape abroad.

"There were striking similarities," said Eklund. "But we have no real way of knowing if they had studied Pearl before Columbine. Although we presume they must have read about it."

It seemed more and more likely that Luke Woodham did indirectly help set off the gun battles in school killing fields across the nation.

In May 1999, a "Schools in the Midst of Crisis" gathering heard this stark warning by one of the nation's foremost child-care experts.

"Nothing has changed since Littleton," Frank Zenere, school psychologist with Miami-Dade County Public Schools, told the education conference. "It isn't that there is more fighting in schools. It is that there is more lethal fighting. In cold terms there is little doubt that factors such as child abuse, ineffective parenting, violence in the home, media violence, poverty, prejudice, substance abuse, and easy access to guns play a major part in sparking the sort of rampages that have haunted this nation's schools since Luke Woodham first marched in the Pearl High School on October 1, 1997.

"A colleague of mine said there are two kinds of schools: one that just experienced this kind of violence and one that is about to experience this kind of violence," said Zenere. "Surveys tell us that from eighteen to twenty-two percent of students need some type of intervention. There aren't enough counselors in the schools to provide that intervention."

Experts say there are four "profiling questions" that might have helped pinpoint Luke Woodham's problems long before he committed his heinous crimes on October 1, 1997.

Is the student able to control or express emotion?

Is he assertive or nonassertive?

Is he predictable or unpredictable?

Is he confident or fearful in his decision-making?

Dan Korem, author of *Suburban Gangs—The Affluent Rebels* and *The Art of Profiling; Reading People Right the First Time*, uses two basic questions to jump start such discussions:

Is actor/comedian Robin Williams controlled or expressive with his emotions? and, *Is Queen Elizabeth controlled or expressive?*

Few people would get these questions wrong, says Korem, but in the real world it's much harder to tell.

Korem says that students performing "random acts" of violent behavior have two major traits in common: They're unpredictable in their actions and they are "extremely fearful in making decisions."

Risk factors for kids who may become "random actors" are a family profile that includes divorce, separation, physical abuse, sexual abuse, or a severely dysfunctional parent.

Then there is a new phenomenon—both parents working when they don't really need to work. In Florida, for example, kids living in $500,000 homes are joining gangs.

Korem reckons that if kids are caught young, then they can be easily saved. But those children need con-

310

cerned parents—protectors before puberty who will
guide them in the right direction.

Inside the much feared Unit 32 of the state penitentiary in Parchman in the early weeks of summer 2000,
Luke Woodham found himself inundated with letters of
support from disaffected teenagers across the country.

Chillingly, many of these teens saw themselves as his
disciples, completely in tune with his reasons for ex-
ploding into violence on that dark day back on October 1, 1997.

Prison authorities kept a close eye on the correspon-
dence, as there were genuine fears Luke Woodham
could elevate himself to the role of messiah to a whole
generation of disaffected teens. Prison authorities were
powerless to stop Woodham getting this so-called "fan
mail." As one staff member at Parchman pointed out,
"We can't stop him getting the letters, but it is truly sad
that there seem to be so many young people out there
who genuinely believe that Luke Woodham had a point
when he murdered three people in cold blood."

On June 1, 2000, Woodham and more than 800
other inmates at Parchman were moved to 400 cells at
Unit 29 of the penitentiary after it had been renovated
from a dormitory to cells.

Woodham—almost twenty years old—was relieved to
get away from the notorious Unit 32, but he was
warned that if he stepped out of line he'd be back
there in a whisper.

Epilogue

The three murders committed by Luke Woodham shocked the nation at first, but they were soon overshadowed by bigger tragedies involving teenagers. Bizarre shooting rampages in small towns in Middle America seem to have become a frighteningly regular occurrence.

The incidence of young people committing acts of violence has become a nationwide issue. Not only are we breeding teens capable of committing horrendous murders, but we are seeing the appalling results of their tormented, twisted minds.

Parents who thought they could safely send their young ones to school are filled with anxiety because this world of violence can explode anywhere, anytime.

But what can we learn from tragedies like Pearl? What should we look out for? Were there clues that were missed? Are there precautions that can be taken? Is there more that we can do?

The stark reality is that unless these questions are properly addressed, then there will be many more victims.

The nation grieves for the families and friends of those who've suffered the loss of their loved ones at Pearl and all the other school killing fields. But these

heartbreaking losses have to send a message to others
to help prevent such tragedies ever happening again.

There is no getting around this simple fact: In coun-
tries with fewer firearms, fewer people die in gun violence. We can no longer ignore the single thread that
ties all the school tragedies of the past five years together.

Just hours after yet another school shooting in late
1999 in Conyers, Georgia, the U.S. Senate narrowly
passed a bill that would require background checks on
sales of firearms at gun shows. It was an unexpected
turn of events. The measure passed by only one vote
after then Vice President Al Gore broke a tie. It passed
primarily because of the deaths and maimings of so
many middle-class kids in recent years.

But that hard-fought victory leaves the nation only
nominally safer. There are still 200 million guns in this
country. There is still a gun lobby that spends millions
every year to fight even minimal gun regulations. It is
still a culture that teaches kids to worship guns.

Stricter gun laws may not have prevented the mayhem at Pearl or the massacre at Columbine, but better
regulations would stop some of the thousands of gun-
related deaths of children every year. The killings at
Pearl High were the first of numerous similar attacks
by students at schools across the nation. More than
two dozen students and teachers have died and more
than sixty-five have been injured in those atrocities.

The emotional damage of those attacks across the
country is difficult to gauge, but there is a growing
perception that school administ   can no longer
guarantee student safety. It seems   in every school
there are students rebelling against s ociety who want
to randomly destroy everything and everyone in their

path. And there is little doubt that this atmosphere of anxiety is not conducive to the learning process in an educational institution.

Today, police and security guards patrol the perimeters of most schools. Many of them are armed to cope with any eventuality. Ten years ago, if a school had a bomb threat, there would be a fire drill, an assembly in the school hall, and then everyone would be marched back into class. Today, every locker is swept clean, every bag, every classroom, every door. No stone can be left unturned. It's a whole new, frightening phenomenon.

The tragic reality in today's violence-riddled America is that for every 100,000 children there is at least one disturbed child prepared to commit a Pearl High–style outrage. School administrators are faced with the nightmare of trying to search out the troublemakers and then deal with them before a tragedy occurs.

School principals have now been briefed about the early warning signs that a student may be troubled or contemplating violence. They are:

- Social withdrawal
- Excessive feelings of isolation and being alone
- Excessive feelings of rejection
- Being a victim of violence
- Feelings of being picked on and persecuted
- Low interest in school and/or poor academic performance
- Expression of violence in writings and drawings
- Uncontrolled anger
- Patterns of impulsive and chronic hitting, intimidating or bullying behaviors

- History of discipline problems
- History of violent or aggressive behavior
- Intolerance of personal differences and/or prejudicial attitudes
- Drug and/or alcohol use
- Affiliation with gangs or groups
- Inappropriate access to, possession of, and use of firearms
- Serious threats of violence
- Past history of violence

Sadly, these days many school officials are relieved when the school year comes to an end with no more than a few prank bomb threats, but no mass violence.

At one of Pearl High's neighboring schools, Forest Hill High, Principal Don Thornton summed it up.

"There's the feeling, 'Thank God it didn't happen to us.' Everyone's like that now. I hope it's something we never get used to. I don't think it's something we will get used to, expect, or tolerate."

Investigator Greg Eklund continues to this day to feel a level of sympathy for Luke Woodham because he had obviously been in an emotional void.

"My impression of Luke was an attention getter. Of course it came out later that he considered himself better than anyone else. He was narcissistic."

While, explained Eklund, Woodham was in many ways one of society's victims, he painted a chilling picture of a teen who was tailor-made for his role as Grant Boyette's "assassin."

"I think the anger inside Luke could actually be converted by someone who knew what they were doing and obviously in this case they did." Added Eklund, "Luke is like a small puppy. If you take that puppy outside to use the bathroom when it messes up, after a while it imprints on that dog that when he has to go to the bathroom he goes outside. You can actually train them and that's the way Luke was. He could actually be trained to do anything."

Luke Woodham is still sitting in his cell in the newly refurbished Unit 29 at Parchman, waiting for his appeal to be argued. He gets few visits and talks to only a handful of other prisoners.

ACKNOWLEDGMENTS

I wish to extend my gratitude to the following individuals, without whose kind support this book would not have been possible:

Rankin County Sheriff's Department Investigator Greg Eklund, current DA Rick Mitchell, Assistant DA Tim Jones, attorney Charles A. Wilson, Andy K., Forrest County Circuit Court Clerk Lou Ellen Adams, Gwen Wilks, Mary James, Chris Soltis, court reporter Sam Reynolds, Susan Garcia, Mario Recillo, Church Sands, and George Burgess of the Pearl Police Department. Also, my literary agent, Piers Murray. And, of course, Paul Dinas, my editor, Karen Haas, and all the kind folk at Kensington Publishing.

MORE BONE-CHILLING STORIES
FROM PINNACLE TRUE CRIME

HORRIFYING TRUE CRIME
FROM PINNACLE BOOKS

HORRIFYING TRUE CRIME
FROM PINNACLE BOOKS